Consumer Watchdogs –
eine Option für die liberalisierten Märkte in Deutschland?

Schriftenreihe des Verbraucherzentrale Bundesverbandes
zur Verbraucherpolitik

Band 5

verbraucherzentrale *Bundesverband*

Consumer Watchdogs –

eine Option für die liberalisierten Märkte
in Deutschland?

BWV · BERLINER WISSENSCHAFTS-VERLAG

Bibliografische Information Der Deutschen Bibliothek

Die Deutsche Bibliothek verzeichnet diese Publikation in der Deutschen Nationalbibliografie; detaillierte bibliografische Daten sind im Internet über http://dnb.ddb.de abrufbar.

ISBN 3-8305-1033-0

Herausgeber:
Verbraucherzentrale Bundesverband e.V.
Markgrafenstraße 66 · 10969 Berlin
Tel. (030) 258 00-0 · Fax (030) 258 00-218
info@vzbv.de · www.vzbv.de

Der vorliegende Text wurde im Auftrag des Verbraucherzentrale Bundesverbandes e.V. erstellt. Die von den Autoren vertretenen Auffassungen geben nicht zwangsläufig die Auffassung des Verbraucherzentrale Bundesverbands wieder.

© 2005 BWV · BERLINER WISSENSCHAFTS-VERLAG
Axel-Springer-Straße 54 B · 10117 Berlin

Printed in Germany. Alle Rechte, auch die des Nachdrucks von Auszügen, der photomechanischen Wiedergabe und der Übersetzung, vorbehalten.

Geleitwort

Am 27. September 2004 war die Britische Botschaft in Berlin Gastgeber der Tagung „'Consumer Watchdogs' – Ein Modell für die liberalisierten Märkte in Deutschland?". Ich danke dem Verbraucherzentrale Bundesverband e.V. und dem Deutschen Mieterbund für die Organisation dieser Veranstaltung. Dafür zu sorgen, dass Großbritannien eine gute Verbraucherschutzordnung hat, ist ein zentrales Anliegen der britischen Regierung.

Die Veranstaltung im vergangenen Jahr hat einen sehr nützlichen Gedanken- und Erfahrungsaustausch bewirkt. Großbritannien hat sich bei der Erarbeitung seiner Verbraucherschutzstrategie „A Fair Deal For All – Extending Competitive Markets: Empowered Consumer, Successful Business" (2005) [auf Deutsch etwa: Ein faires Geschäft für alle – Mehr Wettbewerb auf den Märkten: gestärkte Verbraucher, erfolgreiche Unternehmen] auf einen internationalen Vergleich von Verbraucherschutzvorschriften gestützt.

Die britische Verbraucherschutzstrategie macht deutlich, dass die Verbraucherschutzordnung auf das 21. Jahrhundert zugeschnitten sein muss. Sie soll dem Verbraucher angemessenen Schutz bieten, gleichzeitig aber auch ausgewogen sein und nicht zu einer Überregulierung führen. Die Intervention der Regierung sollte sich auf das zur Realisierung unserer Ziele notwendige Minimum beschränken.

Die britische Regierung ist überzeugt, dass Verbraucherschutz am besten dadurch erreicht wird, die Märkte zu öffnen und den Wettbewerb zu stärken. Die Verbraucher haben so den Vorteil, sich informieren und zwischen den Waren und Dienstleistungen verschiedener Anbieter wählen zu können. Was den weitgehend deregulierten britischen Energiemarkt angeht, hat *Energywatch*, einer der bei dem Seminar vertretenen ‚Consumer Watchdogs', geschätzt, dass die Verbraucher in Großbritannien rund eine Milliarde britische Pfund pro Jahr an Strom- und Gaskosten sparen können, indem sie zum billigsten Anbieter wechseln.

Offene, wettbewerbsorientierte Märkte nützen auch den Unternehmen, denn sie fördern Innovation, Effizienz und Kundenorientierung – und das macht die Unternehmen auf der internationalen Bühne wettbewerbsfähiger. Das Europäische Grünbuch zu Dienstleistungen von allgemeinem wirtschaftlichem Interesse stellte fest, dass die bis dato erfolgte Öffnung der Versorgungsdienstleistungsmärkte zu niedrigeren Preisen für die Verbraucher geführt hat, und dass durch die Öffnung des Netzdienstleistungsmarktes in Europa eine Million neue Arbeitsplätze entstanden sind.

Aber die Öffnung der Versorgungsnetze bringt auch neue Herausforderungen mit sich, zum Beispiel dabei, die Sozial- und Umweltstandards, die wir in Europa haben wollen, weiterhin zu erfüllen. Wenn die Verbraucher die Möglichkeit haben, sich zu informieren und auf wettbewerbsorientieren Märkten zwischen verschiedenen Angeboten zu wählen, stärkt das die Macht der Verbraucher. Verbraucher, die über ihre Rechte und Pflichten Bescheid wissen, sind besser in der Lage, von den Vorteilen einer größeren Auswahl zu profitieren.

An dieser Stelle können die Watchdogs eine wichtige Rolle übernehmen. Zwar kommt auch den Regulierungsbehörden eine bedeutende Funktion zu, aber in der Regel haben sie einen gesetzlich festgelegten Aufgabenbereich, der über den Schutz von Verbraucherinteressen hinausgeht. Die parallel zu den sektorspezifischen Regulierern arbeitenden Watchdogs können einen wichtigen Beitrag zum Verbraucherschutz leisten. Durch Beratung und Information können sie die Verbraucher in die Lage versetzen, Probleme und Beschwerdegründe zu erkennen und dagegen vorzugehen. Dazu gehört auch, die Verbraucher zu ermutigen und sie dabei zu unterstützen, sich direkt mit den Unternehmen auseinanderzusetzen. Watchdogs führen unabhängige Untersuchungen durch, führen Kampagnen im Namen von Verbrauchern und beraten und informieren die Regierung und die Regulierer über die Meinungen der Verbraucher, ihre Forderungen und Bedürfnisse.

Die Art und Weise, wie Watchdogs die besten Ergebnisse für die Verbraucher erzielen können, entwickelt sich weiter. Nach dem ‚UK Enterprise Act 2002' [Unternehmensgesetz] können bestimmte Verbraucherorganisationen, die in direktem Kontakt zu den Verbrauchern stehen, im Namen der von ihnen vertretenen Verbraucher eine Super-Beschwerde bei der Regulierungsbehörde einreichen. In Großbritannien haben die Watchdogs *Energywatch* und *Watervoice* die Befugnis, Super-Beschwerden einzulegen.

Die britische Regierung ist der Auffassung, dass auch in Zukunft weiter Bedarf an einer Interessenvertretung der Verbraucher auf den Versorgungsmärkten – zum Beispiel für Energie, Wasser, Post und Telekommunikation – bestehen wird und sie hat sich damit befasst, wie die Verbraucherschutzordnung weiter angepasst werden kann, damit sie den Bedürfnissen der Verbraucher im 21. Jahrhundert bestmöglich entspricht.

Mit *Consumer Direct* hat die britische Regierung nun eine erste Anlaufstelle für Verbraucher eingerichtet, die per Telefon oder Internet zu erreichen ist. *Consumer Direct* hat die Aufgabe, Verbrauchern in ganz Großbritannien eine qualitativ hochwertige Verbraucherberatung zu bieten. Auch die Verbraucherorganisationen können *Consumer Direct* als Kanal nutzen, um Informationen an die Verbraucher weiterzugeben.

Längerfristig hat die britische Regierung die Einrichtung eines *National Utilities Consumer Council (NUCC)* [Nationaler Versorgungsdienste-Verbraucherrat] vorgeschlagen, der die Verbraucherrechte in einer ganzen Reihe von Sektoren vertreten soll. So könnten Synergien in Verbraucherorganisationen nutzbar gemacht werden, und dies wäre auch eine angemessene Antwort auf die Bildung von Multi-Versorgungsanbietern wie zum Beispiel *Centrica*. Die NUCC-Initiative sieht auch die Schaffung Alternativer Streitbeilegungsmechanismen wie zum Beispiel unabhängige Ombudsmänner vor, die sich komplizierterer Probleme und Streitfälle annehmen sollen, die nicht mit Hilfe des Consumer Direct-Informationsdienstes gelöst werden konnten. Diese langfristige Strategie wird in dem Bericht „Consumer Representation in the regulated Industries" [Vertretung von Verbraucherinteressen in den regulierten Wirtschaftszweigen] im zweiten Teil dieser Veröffentlichung näher beschrieben.

Sir Peter Torry
Britischer Botschafter in Deutschland

Vorwort

Großbritannien ist das Land in Europa, das die Liberalisierung von Leistungen der Daseinsvorsorge am entschiedensten vorangetrieben hat. Hierbei hat man die Erfahrung gemacht, dass die Märkte keineswegs von sich aus effiziente und kundengerechte Leistungen hervorbringen. Um die Interessen der Verbraucher in liberalisierten Märkten gegenüber den Unternehmen durchzusetzen, wurden daher Consumer Watchdogs eingerichtet. Die *„Watchdogs"* sind spezialisierte Verbraucherorganisationen für die Sektoren Energie, Telekommunikation, Post, Eisenbahn und Wasser. Sie nehmen gegenüber den Unternehmen die Rechte der Verbraucher wahr und setzen sich aufgrund ihrer Marktkenntnis politisch für eine verbrauchergerechte Regulierung ein.

Der Verbraucherzentrale Bundesverband und der Deutsche Mieterbund haben am 27. September 2004 mit ihrer gemeinsamen Tagung Consumer Watchdogs die britischen Erfahrungen in die wirtschaftspolitische Diskussion eingebracht. Die Tagung fand in der britischen Botschaft in Berlin statt. Vertreter der Watchdogs für Energie, Post und Wasserversorgung erläuterten das britische Konzept aus erster Hand. Von deutscher Seite befanden sich unter den Referenten und Diskutanten der hessische Wirtschaftsminister Alois Rhiel, der Präsident der Regulierungsbehörde für Post und Telekommunikation, Matthias Kurth, sowie Vertreter aller Fraktionen des deutschen Bundestages. Die Tagung bot damit auch ein ausgezeichnetes Forum, um den verbraucherpolitischen Reformbedarf bei der Novellierung des Energiewirtschaftsrechts deutlich zu machen. Das Energiewirtschaftsgesetz wurde inzwischen verabschiedet. Das britische Modell einer wirksamen institutionellen Regelung zur Vertretung der Verbraucherrechte fand hierin keine Berücksichtigung. Die Verankerung der Verbraucherrechte bei der Regulierung des Energiemarktes wird deshalb auf der Tagesordnung bleiben. Die in diesem Band gemachten Vorschläge zur Schaffung von mehr Verbraucherrechten und mehr Wettbewerb dürfen daher nicht aus dem Auge verloren werden.

Die vorliegende Dokumentation gibt im ersten Teil die Vorträge und Diskussionen der Veranstaltung wieder; im zweiten Teil enthält sie die Evaluation des britischen Watchdog-Systems, welche das britische Department of Trade and Industry im Juli 2004 vorgelegt hat.

Prof. Dr. Edda Müller
Vorstand
Verbraucherzentrale Bundesverband

Inhaltsverzeichnis

Erster Abschnitt:
Consumer Watchdogs – eine Option für die liberalisierten Märkte in Deutschland?[1] 13

  I. Was kann Deutschland lernen? 13
     Edda Müller

 II. Hohe Energiepreise – eine Belastung für Haushalte
     und Binnenkonjunktur 17
     Franz-Georg Rips

III. Die Liberalisierung „regulierter Märkte" und die Vertretung
     der Verbraucherinteressen 20
     Helmut Voelzkow

 IV. Wettbewerbsprobleme im Strommarkt:
     die Sicht der Monopolkommission 34
     Sabine Streb

  V. Regulierung des Strom- und Gasmarktes
     und Verbraucherinteressen 44
     Alois Rhiel

 VI. Die Rolle des „Council of European Energy Regulators"
     bei der Durchsetzung von Verbraucherinteressen
     im liberalisierten Markt 46
     Jorge Vasconcelos

---

[1] Dieser Abschnitt dokumentiert die gemeinsame Tagung des Verbraucherzentrale Bundesverbandes und des Deutschen Mieterbundes „Consumer Watchdogs – eine Option für die liberalisierten Märkte in Deutschland?" vom 27.09.2004 in Berlin. Die Tagungsbeiträge wurden für die vorliegende Publikation überarbeitet und ergänzt.

Inhaltsverzeichnis

VII. Representing consumers' interests in the liberalised gas
and electricity markets – the British model 50
Edward Blades

VIII. The watchdogs: WaterVoice 56
Sheila Reiter

IX. The watchdogs: Postwatch 61
Gregor McGregor

X. The watchdogs: Energywatch 66
Allan Asher

XI. Podiumsdiskussion: Die britischen Consumer Watchdogs –
eine Option für Deutschland?[1] 72

Zweiter Abschnitt:
Consumer Representation in Regulated Industries
A report by the Department of Trade and Industry und HM Treasury 83

Anhang
Vertretung von Verbraucherinteressen in regulierten Märkten –
Informationen zur Situation in Großbritannien und Deutschland 133

Die Autoren 137

---

1   Dokumentation: Anja Dobrodinsky

Erster Abschnitt

Consumer Watchdogs – eine Option für die liberalisierten Märkte in Deutschland?

I. Was kann Deutschland lernen?

Edda Müller

Die Bundesregierung hat einen – nicht nur aus unserer Sicht – völlig unzureichenden und überdies verspäteten Gesetzentwurf zur Regulierung des liberalisierten Strom- und Gasmarktes vorgelegt. Dieser Gesetzentwurf ist derzeit im Gesetzgebungsverfahren. Wir wollen nun, dass die deutsche Politik von der britischen Politik lernt. Die britische Regierung hat erst kürzlich wieder mit einem breit angelegten Konsultationsprozess für eine verbraucherpolitische Strategie ein hohes verbraucherpolitisches Engagement bewiesen. Der Titel des Konsultationspapiers ist bemerkenswert und bringt auch unser verbraucherpolitisches Credo auf den Punkt. Der Titel lautet: „Competitive markets – empowered consumers – successful business!" Gestärkte Verbraucher und eine erfolgreiche Wirtschaft sind eben kein Nullsummenspiel, wie viele Politiker in Deutschland immer noch zu glauben scheinen. Das Gegenteil ist der Fall.

Großbritannien ist in Europa das Vorreiterland bei der Liberalisierung öffentlicher und privater Versorgungsmonopole. Die britische Regierung und der britische Gesetzgeber haben gezeigt, dass die Liberalisierung netzgebundener Märkte nichts mit einer staatlichen „laisser-faire Politik" zu tun hat, sondern einer wirksamen staatlichen Regulierung bedarf. Im Vergleich zur deutschen Debatte ist bemerkenswert, dass Großbritannien nicht nur für wirkungsvolle staatliche Regulierungsbehörden gesorgt hat, sondern zugleich für die Institutionalisierung einer „Gegenmacht", Kontrollinstanz und Anlaufstelle für die Belange der privaten Verbraucher. So wurden die Kompetenzen und die Finanzierung der britischen *consumer watchdogs* jeweils im *Utilities Act* rechtlich abgesichert.

Der britische Gesetzgeber hat also im Interesse der gesamten Volkswirtschaft die notwendige Distanz zu den betroffenen Wirtschaftsunternehmen gewahrt, und er hat zugleich für einen Anwalt der Nachfrageseite des Marktes, das heißt der Millionen Verbraucher, gesorgt. Demgegenüber ist die deutsche „Liberalisierungspraxis" – zumindest hinsichtlich des aktuellen Themas der Liberalisierung des Strom- und Gasmarktes – durch eine Schonung der big players in der Wirtschaft und eine vollständige Ignoranz gegenüber den Bedürfnissen und Interessen der Verbraucher gekennzeichnet. Vordergründiges Zeichen hierfür ist die Tatsache, dass das für die Regulierung des Strom- und Gasmarktes zuständige Bundesministerium für Wirtschaft und Arbeit trotz einer lebhaften Mediendiskussion über die Verbraucherpreise den deutschen Verbraucherverbänden – die wir als Dachorganisation repräsentieren – kein Gesprächsangebot gemacht hat.

Unser zentrales Thema heute ist die wirksame Regulierung des deutschen Strom- und Gasmarktes und die solide Berücksichtigung der Verbraucherinteressen in einem rechtlichen Ordnungsrahmen. Deutschland hat bei der Liberalisierung der Strom- und Gasmärkte im Vergleich zu anderen europäischen Ländern einen Sonderweg eingeschlagen. 1998 wurde der Markt vollständig liberalisiert. Die Konditionen für den Übergang in den Wettbewerb wurden in freiwilligen Vereinbarungen der privaten Wirtschaftsakteure festgelegt. Der Staat wollte sich heraushalten. Merkwürdigerweise ist den verantwortlichen Politikern nie in den Sinn gekommen, dass die gegen die Wirtschaftsmacht der ehemaligen Monopolisten in den Markt drängenden Strom- und Gasanbieter und -händler faire Startchancen benötigen und dass die Millionen privaten Haushalte ebenfalls Wirtschaftsakteure sind. Schließlich ist zum einen ihr Nachfrageverhalten entscheidend dafür, ob Konkurrenten der ehemaligen Monopolanbieter überhaupt eine Chance im Wettbewerb erhalten. Zum anderen wurde anscheinend nie reflektiert, dass das Preisniveau auf dem Energiemarkt von immenser Bedeutung für die generelle Wettbewerbsfähigkeit der deutschen Wirtschaft und die – in der derzeitigen deutschen Wirtschafts- und Arbeitsmarktsituation – besonders prekäre Binnennachfrage ist.

Der „deutsche Sonderweg" ist – in diesem Punkt sind sich inzwischen alle relevanten Akteure in Deutschland einig – gescheitert. In den sechs Jahren, in denen der Staat auf die Selbstregulierung und „Selbstbeschränkung" von großen Energieanbietern und ihren großen Industriekunden vertraute, wurden aber Fakten geschaffen. Die ehemaligen Gebietsmonopolunternehmen haben ihre Versorgungsgebiete erfolgreich verteidigt. Die vier großen Stromanbieter halten einen Marktanteil von 73 Prozent an der Stromerzeugung und 56 Prozent an der Stromabgabe an die Letztverbraucher. Von der Möglichkeit, den Anbieter zu wechseln, haben in Deutschland nur etwa vier bis fünf Prozent der privaten Haushalte Gebrauch gemacht, gegenüber annähernd 50 Prozent der britischen Privathaushalte. Im Gasbereich ist der Wettbewerb noch gar nicht in die Gänge gekommen.

Die deutschen Strom- und Gaspreise liegen im europäischen Vergleich – vor Steuern – mit an der Spitze. Würde das deutsche Preisniveau an die britischen Verbraucherpreise angeglichen, so ließe sich in Deutschland ein Nachfragevolumen von circa elf Milliarden Euro mobilisieren. Statt in die Kassen der Energiekonzerne zu fließen, könnte ein Großteil dieser Nachfrage in den allgemeinen Konsum gehen und damit für die ersehnte Belebung der Binnennachfrage und die Schaffung neuer Arbeitsplätze sorgen. Für das hohe deutsche Energiepreisniveau wird häufig ins Feld geführt, dass nur finanzkräftige Energieunternehmen und Netzbetreiber die langfristige Versorgungssicherheit garantieren könnten. Auch müsste zur Verteidigung des Energiestandorts Deutschland genügend Investitionskapital angehäuft werden, um in einigen Jahren den Erneuerungsbedarf der deutschen Kraftwerkskapazität zu finanzieren. Auch für den Verbraucherzentrale Bundesverband ist die langfristige Versorgungssicherheit ein hohes Ziel. Kalifornische Verhältnisse wollen wir in Deutschland nicht. Wir wollen ebenso wenig, dass die Abhängigkeit Deutschlands von Energieimporten weiter zunimmt. Was wir aber nicht wollen, ist ein Ordnungsrahmen, der einen echten Leistungswettbewerb verhindert, durch lediglich nachträgliche Kontrollen den Gebietsmonopolisten weiter Zeit lässt, ihre marktbeherrschende Stellung auszubauen und die nicht transparente Kalkulation der Netzentgelte fortsetzt.

Vor allem wollen wir einen Ordnungsrahmen, der die Herstellung fairer Wettbewerbsbedingungen und die Herbeiführung kosten- und leistungsgerechter Energiepreise für die Verbraucher als einen Prozess der Marktoptimierung begreift. Das tatsächliche Geschehen im Privatkundenmarkt muss auch nach der Verabschiedung des Gesetzes und von zahlreichen Verordnungen systematisch beobachtet, Fehlentwicklungen und Problemfälle müssen kontinuierlich in die Regulierungspraxis rückgespiegelt werden. Damit dies geschehen kann, brauchen wir rechtlich abgesicherte institutionelle Vorkehrungen in der Regulierungsbehörde selbst, bei den Energieversorgern und auf Seiten der unabhängigen Verbraucherorganisationen.

Wir fordern:

- die Einrichtung einer auf die Bedürfnisse der Privatkunden und kleinen Gewerbetreibenden spezialisierten Beschlusskammer in der künftigen Regulierungsbehörde,
- verbindliche Vorschriften zur Einrichtung von Beschwerdestellen für die privaten Verbraucher in den die Endkunden beliefernden Strom- und Gasunternehmen sowie regelmäßige Berichtspflichten der Unternehmen gegenüber der Re-

gulierungsbehörde über die Art der Verbraucherbeschwerden und ihr Beschwerdemanagement,

- die Schaffung der Funktion des unabhängigen *consumer watchdog* mit klaren gesetzlich abgesicherten Kompetenzen und Finanzierungsregelungen.

Die Aufgabe der *consumer watchdogs* wäre eine dreifache:

1. Sie sollen den Privatkundenmarkt systematisch beobachten und festgestellte Fehlentwicklungen und Missstände gebündelt an die Regulierungsbehörde herantragen, um auf diese Weise für eine generelle Abhilfe zu sorgen.
2. Sie sollen Anlaufstelle für Verbraucherbeschwerden sein, die von den Beschwerdestellen der Unternehmen abgewiesen oder nicht zufriedenstellend behandelt wurden.
3. Sie sollen als Schlichtungsinstanzen zwischen den Verbrauchern und den Unternehmen wirken sowie im Fall des Scheiterns der Schlichtung besondere Ablehnungsfälle auf dem Klageweg vor den Gerichten klären lassen.

In Deutschland sind unter dem Dach des Verbraucherzentrale Bundesverbands die organisatorischen Voraussetzungen in Gestalt eines flächendeckenden Netzwerkes von Verbraucherberatungsstellen der Verbraucherzentralen und sektoralen Verbraucherverbänden für die Marktbeobachtung und Behandlung von Verbraucherbeschwerden vorhanden. Die notwendige Bündelung von Empfehlungen an die Regulierungsbehörde und die Einleitung von Klagen kann zentral über den Bundesverband geleistet werden. Wir brauchen „nur noch" einen klaren gesetzlichen Auftrag und die Finanzierung, damit das britische „Gegenmachtmodell" der *consumer watchdogs* auch in Deutschland mit Leben erfüllt werden kann.

II. Hohe Energiepreise – eine Belastung für Haushalte und Binnenkonjunktur

Franz-Georg Rips

Die Schaffung eines gerechten Ausgleichs zwischen Wirtschafts- und Verbraucherinteressen auf dem liberalisierten europäischen Binnenmarkt steht heute und in Zukunft im Focus der politischen Debatte. Großbritannien hat dabei auf diesem Gebiet eine Vorreiterrolle gespielt. Was den Energiemarkt und die Beteiligung der Verbraucherschützer betrifft, können wir von unserem europäischen Nachbarn einiges lernen.

In Deutschland leben etwa 50 Millionen Menschen zur Miete. Der Deutsche Mieterbund mit seinen drei Millionen Mitgliedern ist die einzige bundesweit organisierte Interessenvertretung der Mieterschaft und hat ein originäres Interesse daran, sich in den Entscheidungsprozess der Reform des Energiewirtschaftsgesetzes (EnWG) einzubringen und dabei weitestgehend Verbraucherschutzrechte durchzusetzen. Im Übrigen unterscheiden sich die Interessen der Mieter in dieser Frage nicht von denjenigen der selbst nutzenden Wohnungseigentümer.

Wir haben uns mit einer Stellungnahme zum Energiewirtschaftsgesetz bereits „eingemischt" und damit gemeinsam mit dem Verbraucherzentrale Bundesverband einen Schulterschluss aller Privatverbraucher erreicht, um der nach oben offenen Preisspirale auf dem Strom- und Gasmarkt ein Stoppsignal entgegenzusetzen. Unterstützt werden wir dabei von der unternehmerischen Wohnungswirtschaft: Der Bundesverband deutscher Wohnungsunternehmen (GdW) hat sich unserer Auffassung angeschlossen – eine Allianz von Mietern und Vermietern, die nicht alltäglich ist. Sie zeigt jedoch: Das Problem der steigenden Energiepreise belastet das Verhältnis von Mietern und Vermietern – die Grenzen der Kaufkraft der Normalverdiener-Haushalte sind ausgereizt. Hohe Energiekosten mindern den Spielraum für Grundmietenerhöhungen. Geringe Mieten schwächen die Investitionskraft der Wohnungsanbieter, schaden der Bauwirtschaft und stehen dem Ziel einer Beschäftigungsförderung entgegen. Denjenigen, die unsere Kritik an den Belastungen durch hohe Energiepreise als Peanuts und Pfennigfuchserei abqualifizieren, möchte ich schlichte Fakten entgegenhalten: Die Mieter in Deutschland geben insgesamt etwa 41 Milliarden Euro für die Nebenkosten des Wohnens aus. Wenigstens fünf Milliarden, also mehr als zwölf Prozent ließen sich durch verbraucherfreundlichere Regelungen auf den Energiemärkten einsparen.

Die Nebenkosten des Wohnens haben sich längst zu einer zweiten Miete entwickelt. Sie belaufen sich heute bereits durchschnittlich auf ein Drittel der gesamten Wohnkostenbelastung und betragen in vielen Mietverhältnissen bis zu 50 Prozent. Die Betriebskosten des Wohnens sind keine starre Größe. Sie hängen von den Preisentwicklungen, insbesondere auf den Energiemärkten ab. Die deutschen Privathaushalte zahlen im europäischen Vergleich nahezu die höchsten Preise für Strom und Gas. Sie liegen beim Strom mit 12,6 Cent je Kilowattstunde vor Steuern und Abgaben und beim Gas mit 3,9 Cent je Kilowattstunde 50 Prozent über dem jeweiligen britischen Niveau. Nach den Ankündigungen der Energieversorger ist das Ende der Fahnenstange jedoch noch lange nicht erreicht. Wird der Preistreiberei kein Riegel vorgeschoben, wird nach dem Winter 2004 mit der Betriebskostenabrechnung ein böses Erwachen für die Mieterhaushalte kommen.

Bei steigenden Gas-, Strom- und Heizölpreisen fallen für eine 70-Quadratmeter-Wohnung folgende Zusatz-Kosten an:

- Steigt der Gaspreis um zehn Prozent an, sind im Schnitt 55 Euro Mehrkosten zu bezahlen.
- Wird der Strom um fünf Prozent teurer, ist mit 17 Euro mehr zu rechnen.
- Bei den aktuell gegenüber Januar 2004 um 30 Prozent gestiegenen Heizölkosten sind 110 Euro zusätzlich zu bezahlen.

Diese Zahlen beziehen sich auf einen Kleinhaushalt. Für eine 100-Quadratmeter-Familienwohnung summieren sich die Mehrkosten auf rund 280 Euro. Geld, das den Haushalten fehlt und das dringend zur Ankurbelung der Binnenkonjunktur nötig ist. Es ist an der Zeit, dass der Staat seine Verantwortung wahrnimmt. Wir brauchen eine Preisaufsicht, die der willkürlichen Preistreiberei und der Selbstbedienungsmentalität der Energieversorger ein Ende setzt. Viel zu lange wurde ein System geduldet, in dem die Anbieter ihre Gebiets-Monopolstellung ausnutzen und quasi per Handschlag ihre Gewinnmargen vergrößern konnten. Es ist gut, dass wir mit einer Regulierungsbehörde für Strom und Gas das Preiskartell der Energie-Riesen durchbrechen. Es ist gut, dass wir diese Instanz jetzt neu schaffen. Nur – sie darf kein zahnloser Tiger werden. Die geplante Reform des Energiewirtschaftsrechtes weist wesentliche Schwächen auf.

Haupthindernis für einen echten Wettbewerb sind die überhöhten Netzentgelte. Sie machen zum Beispiel 30 bis 40 Prozent des Strompreises aus. Die Netze werden weitgehend von den vier großen Energieversorgern in Deutschland kontrolliert. Über die Preise für die Netznutzung verhindern sie den Einstieg Dritter in den Markt. Dass diese Preise willkürlich festgesetzt werden, wird durch die Bandbreite der Preisgestaltung der Stromriesen deutlich: Die Preise für die Nutzung fremder

Netze schwanken laut der Energie Baden-Württemberg AG (EnBW) in Deutschland bis zu 300 Prozent. Hier muss der Gesetzgeber an mehreren Fronten tätig werden:

1. Die Gebühren müssen vorab genehmigt werden. Es gibt keinen Grund dafür, dass die Verbraucher ungerechtfertigte Monopolgewinne an die Energieunternehmen im Voraus zahlen sollen. Die von der Bundesregierung vorgesehene Prüfung der Plausibilität im Nachhinein reicht nicht aus.
2. Die Grundlagen der Netzgebührenkalkulation müssen gründlich durchleuchtet und die Quersubventionierungen zwischen Netzbetrieb und Stromhandel ausgeschlossen werden. Auch ein Richtpreis, der Anreize zur Preissenkung gibt, würde hier mehr Markttransparenz und Wettbewerb schaffen.
3. Der Netzzugang für den Gasmarkt muss im Gesetz geregelt werden.
4. Die Koppelung des Gaspreises an den Heizölpreis muss beendet werden. Sie ist volkswirtschaftlich schädlich und angesichts der zunehmenden Bedeutung des Energieträgers Gas für Haushaltskunden nicht mehr zeitgemäß. 46 Prozent aller Privathaushalte heizen bereits mit Gas; 76 Prozent der Neubauten werden mittlerweile mit Gasheizungen ausgestattet. Die Bundesregierung ist aufgefordert, die Differenzen zwischen sinkenden Gasbezugspreisen und steigenden Endverbraucherpreisen genau zu prüfen.
5. Wir brauchen mehr Verbrauchermitbestimmung, die institutionalisiert ist. Dies können eine eigene Kammer bei der Regulierungsbehörde und gleichzeitig gestärkte, unabhängige Verbraucherorganisationen sein, die sich auf die jeweiligen Energiemärkte spezialisieren und als zentrale Verbraucherinformations- und Beschwerdestellen fungieren.

Die Lösungsvorschläge der Verbraucherorganisationen sind auf dem Tisch. Wir sind bereit, unser Know-how in ein neues Gesetz mit Biss einzubringen. Großbritannien ist dabei für uns ein Vorbild bei der Liberalisierung der Strom- und Gasmärkte. Mit einer starken Regulierungsbehörde konnten die Netzentgelte deutlich gesenkt werden. Profiteure sind die Endverbraucher, die im europäischen Vergleich die geringsten Preise für Gas und Strom bezahlen. Die Briten haben mit den consumer watchdogs eine Institution geschaffen, die sowohl als Servicestelle für Verbraucher als auch als politische Interessenvertretung auf den Versorgungsmärkten erfolgreich etabliert ist. In den deutschen Energiemarkt kommt nach Jahren der Stagnation durch „verbändevereinbarte" Märkte und closed shops endlich Bewegung. Wir sind an einem Punkt angelangt, an dem wir gemeinsam mit allen politischen Kräften die Eckpfeiler für ein funktionierendes, dem Verbraucherschutz dienendes System setzen können.

III. Die Liberalisierung „regulierter Märkte" und die Vertretung der Verbraucherinteressen

Helmut Voelzkow

I. Einführung

Der internationale Vergleich ist immer wieder für Überraschungen gut. Diese simple These bestätigt sich, wenn die Liberalisierung von „regulierten Märkten" in verschiedenen europäischen Ländern unter die Lupe genommen wird. Der internationale Vergleich ergibt nicht nur gravierende Unterschiede in der Konzeption und Umsetzung der Liberalisierungspolitik, sondern auch in der Organisation einer eigenständigen Vertretung der Verbraucherinteressen.

Folgt man den Verlautbarungen der Politik, dann sollten eigentlich die Verbraucher die Nutznießer der Liberalisierungspolitik sein. Ob aber die Verbraucher tatsächlich von der Liberalisierung profitieren, hängt davon ab, wie die Liberalisierungspolitik aussieht. Wie sich derzeit in Deutschland zeigt, kann das Liberalisierungsprojekt auch danebengehen. Was die Konzeption und Umsetzung der Liberalisierung betrifft, zeigt ein internationaler Vergleich von Deutschland und Großbritannien, dass die in Deutschland gewählten Strategien – diplomatisch formuliert – nicht immer optimal waren. Die Liberalisierungspolitik in Großbritannien hat andere Wege gewählt – mit deutlich besseren Ergebnissen für die Verbraucher. Deshalb besteht in Deutschland aller Anlass, von den britischen Nachbarn zu lernen. Auch was die Vertretung der Verbraucherinteressen in regulierten Märkten angeht, ist Großbritannien weiter als Deutschland.

In diesem Beitrag wird zunächst die Frage behandelt, welche Probleme mit einer Liberalisierung „regulierter Märkte" zwangsläufig verbunden sind (Abschnitt 1). Sodann wird anhand einiger aktueller Beispiele gezeigt, dass die Liberalisierungspolitik in Deutschland zu Fehlentwicklungen geführt hat, die nun dringend durch Reformen behoben werden müssen (Abschnitt 2). Ein Vergleich der Liberalisierungspolitik in Deutschland und in Großbritannien liefert erste Hinweise, wie solche Reformen aussehen könnten (Abschnitt 3). Der internationale Vergleich macht zweierlei deutlich: Wenn die Liberalisierung dem Verbraucher dienen soll, dann ist staatliche Verantwortung (in Form von schlagkräftigen Regulierungsbehörden) zur Sicherstellung der Funktionsfähigkeit des Marktes unabdingbar. Zudem lehren die britischen Erfahrungen, dass das Verbraucherinteresse in der Liberalisierungspolitik auch institutionell abgesichert werden muss. Großbritannien hat vorgemacht, wie eine solche Vertretung der Verbraucherinteressen in der Liberalisierung von „regulierten Märkten" aussehen kann. Erste Schlussfolgerungen, die aus dem internationalen Vergleich für die deutsche Politik abgeleitet werden können, schließen den Beitrag ab (Abschnitt 4).

1. Die Probleme der Liberalisierung „regulierter" Märkte

Zunächst ist zu klären, was „regulierte Märkte" überhaupt sind. Eigentlich sind ja alle Märkte reguliert, zumindest insofern, als jede wirtschaftliche Transaktion von Marktteilnehmern eine rechtliche Grundlage hat. Solche generellen Regulierungen, die letztlich alle „freien" Märkte gleichermaßen betreffen, dienen vielfach auch dem Verbraucherschutz, wie sich beispielsweise im allgemeinen Wettbewerbsrecht zeigt. Aber wenn heute über „regulierte Märkte" gesprochen wird, ist etwas anderes gemeint. Mit diesem Begriff werden Dienstleistungssektoren bezeichnet, deren Gemeinsamkeit darin besteht, dass sie jeweils über eine spezifische Netzinfrastruktur verfügen. Alle Unternehmen, die in diesen Wirtschaftsbranchen ihre Leistungen anbieten, hängen an einem gemeinsamen Netz. Konkret werden mit dem Begriff der „regulierten Märkte" folgende Wirtschaftsbranchen zusammengefasst:

1. Der Telekommunikationssektor (Telefon): Der Telekommunikationssektor stützt sich auf das Telefonnetz (Festnetz). Für die Alternativen zum klassischen Festnetztelefon (Mobiltelefon) werden wie für die elektronischen Kommunikationsdienste heutzutage zwar auch drahtlose Übertragungswege genutzt, aber auch diese Alternativen stützen sich auf ein verzweigtes Netz in Form von Satelliten und zahlreichen Übertragungsmasten.

2. Der Energiesektor (Strom, Gas): Die Energieversorgung der Unternehmen und der privaten Haushalte läuft ebenfalls über eine komplexe Netzinfrastruktur. So ist heute praktisch jeder Haushalt an das Stromnetz angeschlossen, viele Haushalte verfügen zudem über einen Gasleitungsanschluss.

3. Der traditionelle Postsektor: Auch hier ist die Vorstellung eines gemeinsamen Netzes präsent, verstanden als einer Infrastruktur von Briefkästen und Poststellen, die dem Bürger beziehungsweise dem Kunden den Zugang zu einem öffentlichen Kommunikationssystem erschließen.

4. Der Eisenbahnsektor: Züge fahren bekanntlich auf Schienen. Beim Eisenbahnsektor handelt sich also um ein Personen- und Gütertransportsystem, das auf einem gemeinsamen Schienennetz aufbaut, auch wenn dieses Schienensystem von mehreren Unternehmen genutzt wird.

5. Die Wasserversorgung: Auch die Wasserversorgung einschließlich der Abwasserentsorgung wird über ein komplexes Rohrleitungssystem abgewickelt, auf das die Leistungsanbieter und ihre Endkunden zugreifen können müssen.

Über all diese Wirtschaftsbranchen lässt sich sagen, dass sie früher einmal entweder Teil der staatlichen Verwaltung waren oder zumindest als staatsnahe Privatwirtschaft organisiert und reglementiert wurden. Dies gilt für das Telefon, früher ein Monopol der Post, und für die Deutsche Bundesbahn, ebenfalls ein Staatsunternehmen. Einige dieser Dienstleistungssektoren laufen auch heute noch unter öffentlicher Regie, wie sich in Deutschland am Beispiel der Wasserversorgung zeigt. Im Unterschied zur Post und zur Deutschen Bundesbahn, die als staatseigene Unternehmen geführt wurden, lag die Energieversorgung mit Strom und Gas zwar immer schon in der Hand von privaten Unternehmen, aber diese Unternehmen verfügten über rechtlich abgesicherte und geschützte Gebietsmonopole. Der Wettbewerb war auch in der Strom- und Gaswirtschaft durch die staatliche Rahmensetzung außer Kraft gesetzt. Dafür mussten die Energieversorgungsunternehmen – im Gegenzug für diese Ausschaltung des Wettbewerbs – zahlreiche staatliche Anforderungen bei ihren Dienstleistungen berücksichtigen. Der Staat war damit in den genannten netzverbundenen Wirtschaftssektoren – direkt über staatseigene Unternehmen oder indirekt durch rechtlich abgesicherte Gebietsmonopole – in einer Produzentenrolle. Über die öffentlichen oder staatlich geschützten Monopole war der Staat allgegenwärtig. Der Wettbewerb durch private Konkurrenzangebote war ausgeschaltet.

Der Sachverhalt, dass der Staat in den Wirtschaftssektoren mit einer Netzinfrastruktur als der alleinige Anbieter oder zumindest als Regulierungsinstanz auftrat, war auch theoretisch begründbar. Weil die Dienstleistungen, um die es hier geht, allesamt über technische Netzstrukturen angeboten werden, kann – so die ökonomische Theorie – ein „natürliches Monopol" vorliegen. Von einem „natürlichen Monopol" wird dann gesprochen, wenn ein einziger Anbieter den relevanten Markt kostengünstiger bedienen kann als mehrere Anbieter. Es wäre im Fall eines natürlichen Monopols ökonomisch unsinnig und letztlich auch unbezahlbar, parallele Netzinfrastrukturen aufzubauen. Um Versorgungslücken (beispielsweise in abgelegenen Regionen) zu vermeiden und um sicherzustellen, dass die erforderlichen Investitionen in diese kostenintensive Netzinfrastruktur erfolgen, ist früher gewissermaßen aus dem natürlichen Monopol das öffentliche Monopol abgeleitet worden.[1] Die öffentlichen Monopole wurden in der Vergangenheit damit begründet,

---

1 Vgl. Knieps (2004, S. 11).

dass nur der Staat in der Lage sei, ein solches flächendeckendes Angebot von Netzinfrastrukturen in einer verbrauchergerechten Quantität und Qualität bereitzustellen.

Heute sieht man dies bekanntlich anders. Die ehemaligen öffentlichen Monopole sollen liberalisiert und damit in den privaten Sektor überführt werden. Seit Jahren sind praktisch alle entwickelten Industrieländer dabei, ihre ehemals staatseigen oder staatsnah organisierten Netzsektoren in private Marktstrukturen zu überführen.

Allerdings muss es sich bei diesen Märkten, die nun Schritt für Schritt liberalisiert werden, auch in Zukunft um „regulierte Märkte" handeln. Dies ist so, weil die Problematik des „natürlichen Monopols" auch bei einer Liberalisierung bestehen bleibt. Die Unternehmen könnten, sofern sie diese Netze exklusiv besitzen, den Zugang zu ihrer Netzinfrastruktur dazu missbrauchen, sich missliebige Konkurrenz vom Hals zu halten. Mit ihrer Netzinfrastruktur könnten sie den Wettbewerb behindern, um die Preise zu ihrem Vorteil hoch zu halten.

Wie die bisherigen Erfahrungen zeigen, versuchen viele Unternehmen auch tatsächlich, das Netz und den Zugang zum Netz strategisch zu nutzen. Bei Strom und Gas sind es die Leitungen, bei der Telekom ist es zumindest das Festnetz und bei der Bahn ist es das Schienennetz. Immer sind die Nachfolgeunternehmen, die im Zuge der Liberalisierung aus den ehemaligen öffentlichen oder staatlich geschützten Monopolen hervorgehen, versucht, die Konditionen zu bestimmen, zu denen neue Wettbewerber ihre Netzinfrastruktur benutzen dürfen. Wer das Netz hat, hat den Markt.

Würden die netzgebundenen Dienstleistungen nicht reguliert, dann würden die öffentlichen oder staatlich geschützten Monopole – aufgrund des Fortbestandes der Eigenschaft eines „natürlichen Monopols" – durch privatwirtschaftliche Monopole ersetzt. Damit wäre dann aber keinem gedient. Allenfalls die neuen privaten Monopolisten könnten frohlocken, weil sie sich die Märkte der ehemaligen öffentlichen oder öffentlich geschützten Monopole einverleiben können. Das eigentliche Ziel der Liberalisierung aber, die ja eigentlich für die Bürger und Verbraucher Vorteile bringen soll, wie in der Begründung der Liberalisierungspolitik ständig behauptet wird, würde systematisch verfehlt.

Die Überführung von Dienstleistungssektoren, die früher im Rahmen der „öffentlichen Daseinsvorsorge" erbracht wurden, in neue Sektoren mit einer privatwirtschaftlich organisierten Bereitstellung kann sich deshalb nicht auf eine einfache De-Regulierung beschränken. Vielmehr muss die Liberalisierung eine Re-Regulierung einschließen. Dies wird in der öffentlichen Diskussion, die von den Vorzügen des Marktes überzeugt ist und staatliche Bürokratie ablehnt, häufig übersehen. Gerade die Liberalisierung ehemaliger staatlicher Monopolmärkte zieht einen hohen Bedarf an Regulierung nach sich. Die marktwirtschaftliche Öffnung durch Aufhebung eines öffentlichen Monopols muss mit zahlreichen Regulierungen für den „neuen Markt" verbunden werden, damit dieser Markt auch tatsächlich im Interesse der Bürger und Verbraucher greifen kann. Vor allem muss verhindert werden, dass die Märkte, die durch Liberalisierung für private Anbieter geöffnet werden, in ein privates Monopol „umkippen".

Weil die Liberalisierung „regulierter Märkte" im Interesse der Bürger und Verbraucher nicht auf eine Übernahme ehemaliger Staatsaufgaben durch private Unternehmen reduziert werden darf, bleibt der Staat auch nach der Liberalisierung im Spiel. Aber er ändert seine Rolle. Die Liberalisierung ist mit einer Funktionsverschiebung des Staates verbunden: Der Staat gibt mit der Liberalisierung seine unmittelbare Produzentenrolle auf. Aber er muss so etwas wie eine Gewährleistungsrolle übernehmen, wenn das Liberalisierungsprojekt im Interesse der Bürger und Verbraucher gelingen soll. Die Aufgaben und Zuständigkeiten zwischen Staat und Markt werden neu zugeschnitten. Es kommt zu einer politisch verantworteten Ausdifferenzierung von Politik, Management und operativen Tätigkeiten, die eine Übertragung der Produzentenrolle auf private Unternehmen einschließt, aber die Gewährleistungsrolle muss in staatlicher Hand bleiben. Die Liberalisierung ehemals staatseigener oder staatsnaher Sektoren muss deshalb immer auch eine Rückbesinnung auf die staatlichen Kernaufgaben einschließen. Wenn diese Grundsätze missachtet werden, kann das Liberalisierungsprojekt schief gehen.

2. Fehlentwicklungen der Liberalisierung am Beispiel des Energiesektors in Deutschland

Deutschland hat den nationalen Strommarkt bereits 1998 dem Wettbewerb geöffnet. Die monopolistische Ordnung der Elektrizitätsversorgung, die seit den Anfangszeiten dieser Branche bestand[2], wurde 1998 durch ein neues Regelsystem abgelöst, das den Markt öffnen sollte. Dieser Reform waren zahlreiche Konflikte vorausgegangen. Die deutsche Stromwirtschaft hatte lange Zeit versucht, die Liberalisierung abzuwehren. Und als sie die Marktöffnung nicht mehr verhindern konnte, hat die deutsche Stromwirtschaft auf die konkrete Art und Weise der Liberalisierung Einfluss genommen.[3] Mit der großen Strukturreform Ende der 1990er

---

2 Zur historischen Entwicklung der deutschen Elektrizitätswirtschaft vgl. Hughes (1983).
3 Vgl. dazu den Beitrag von Voß (2000).

Jahre aber sind die Probleme nicht aus der Welt geschafft worden. Im Gegenteil, was die Regulierung des Energiesektors (Strom- und Gasmarkt) betrifft, erleben wir derzeit in Deutschland eine sehr heftige und äußerst kontroverse Diskussion, die Anlass gibt, die gewählten Liberalisierungsstrategien grundsätzlich zu überdenken.

Strom kostet in Deutschland heute viel mehr als in anderen europäischen Ländern. Ende 2004 kündigte Deutschlands größter Stromversorger RWE noch eine weitere Preiserhöhung für die Endkunden um fünf Prozent an. Die Konkurrenz zog sofort nach. Vattenfall will um sechs Prozent erhöhen, Ruhrgas fordert vier Prozent mehr ein und Erdgas Südsachsen denkt über eine Preiserhöhung von fünf Prozent nach.[4] Diese angekündigten Preiserhöhungen sorgen aktuell für politische Unruhe, denn so schlecht geht es den Energieversorgern eigentlich nicht. Die Renditen der Unternehmen liegen im zweistelligen Bereich. Die Energieversorger schieben zwar alle möglichen Begründungen für ihre Preiserhöhungen vor, aber die Öffentlichkeit bleibt zu recht kritisch. Die Unternehmen der Energiewirtschaft behaupten, dass politisch gewollte Abgaben und die steigenden Rohstoffpreise die Preiserhöhungen unvermeidlich machen. Aber es sieht so aus, als hätten die Energieunternehmen diesmal mit ihrer Preispolitik überzogen. Allein die Ankündigung der Preiserhöhung hat erneut den Ruf nach einer staatlichen Preiskontrolle provoziert.

Das Bundeswirtschaftsministerium versucht zwar noch, die Wogen zu glätten und die Verbraucher (Industrie und private Haushalte) zu beschwichtigen: Bald solle eine Energie-Regulierungsbehörde für Preissenkungen sorgen und den Verbraucher entlasten. Was dabei nicht erwähnt wird, ist der kuriose Sachverhalt, dass diese neue Regulierungsbehörde gar nicht auf deutsche Initiative hin, sondern nur aufgrund des Drucks aus Brüssel eingerichtet wird.[5] Nach einer europäischen Richtlinie („Beschleunigungsrichtlinie" vom 26. Juni 2003, Richtlinie 96/92/EG) muss Deutschland „eine oder mehrere zuständige Stellen mit der Aufgabe als Regulierungsbehörde" betrauen (Art. 23 Abs. 1 Richtlinie). Damit hat die Europäische Union den bisherigen deutschen Weg der Liberalisierung der Elektrizitätswirtschaft, der sich auf Vereinbarungen der Verbände stützt, zu einem Auslaufmodell gemacht.

---

4 Zahlenangaben von Cerstin Gammelin, „Deutscher Strom soll teuer bleiben" in „Die Zeit" vom 9.9.2004, S. 36.
5 Auf die Vorstellungen und Ziele der europäischen Liberalisierungspolitik geht der Beitrag von Jorge Vasconcelos (in diesem Band) noch näher ein.

Aber es bleibt fraglich, ob die neue Regulierungsbehörde tatsächlich leisten kann, was da in Aussicht gestellt wird. Nach Einschätzung der Kritiker (auch der Verbraucherverbände) dürften die neu verfassten 118 Paragrafen des Energiewirtschaftsrechts, die derzeit zur Entscheidung anstehen, die gewünschte Korrektur der Preistreiberei des Oligopols nicht leisten können. Im Gegenteil, nach Einschätzung vieler Kritiker kommt die Energiemarktreform viel zu spät und viel zu halbherzig.

Verzögerungen in der Umsetzung der Brüsseler Auflagen haben die neue Welle der Preiserhöhungen erst ermöglicht. Die Energieversorger wollen sich, solange es noch geht, zusätzlichen Spielraum verschaffen, bevor die künftige Regulierungsbehörde überhaupt anfangen kann, über verordnete Preissenkungen nachzudenken. Nach Einschätzung der Verbraucherorganisationen dürften Industrie, Gewerbe und private Verbraucher trotz der geplanten gesetzlichen Neuregelungen auf den überhöhten Preisen sitzen bleiben. Die Kritiker bemängeln, dass auch die vorgesehenen Neuregelungen keine marktwirtschaftlichen Anreize enthalten, die Preise zu senken.

Die in Deutschland angekündigte Reform wird die Situation der Verbraucher zumindest kurzfristig nicht wesentlich ändern. Das eigentliche Problem besteht darin, dass sich noch keine Methode zur Feststellung von fairen Netzpreisen etabliert hat. Was fehlt, ist die Herstellung von Transparenz. Andere Länder trennen den Netzbetrieb von den Kraftwerken, nur die deutsche Energiewirtschaft beharrt auf ihrer sogenannten „integrierten Versorgung" – ohne die gebotene Trennung von Netzbetrieb und Kraftwerken. Es geht ihr letztlich um ihr letztes Privileg. Die Verteidiger des Monopols brauchen diese Intransparenz. Deshalb brandmarken sie die Herstellung von Transparenz als neuen „Regulierungswahn". Damit wird gegen eine Regulierung polemisiert, die in anderen Ländern – im Interesse der Industrie und der Verbraucher – längst gängige Praxis ist. Da mittlerweile der gemeinsame europäischen Binnenmarkt Realität ist, liefern die deutschen Unternehmen der Energiewirtschaft sogar unfreiwillig selbst den Beweis, dass sie auch mit anderen Rahmenbedingungen zurechtkämen: Sie arbeiten auch in den „regulierten Märkten" der Nachbarländer durchaus mit Gewinn, wie beispielsweise das Engagement von E.ON und RWE in Großbritannien zeigt.

Im Unterschied zum Strommarkt ist die Liberalisierung des Gasmarktes in Deutschland noch mitten in der Eingangsphase der Liberalisierung. Hier droht aber dieselbe Fehlentwicklung wie auf dem Strommarkt. Ein Wettbewerb findet praktisch nicht statt. Die Verbraucher als Endkunden haben praktisch keine Alternative. Die lokalen Märkte sind zumeist in der Hand eines einzigen Gasversorgers. Der überregionale Gasmarkt wird von einem Großunternehmen beherrscht: Die Ruhrgas AG erreicht einen Marktanteil von 60 Prozent des gesamten deutschen Gasabsatzes.

Die größten Konkurrenten erreichen nur sehr geringe Marktanteile: RWE Gas und BEB liegen jeweils um die zehn Prozent. Die Wettbewerbsproblematik ist mit der Situation auf dem deutschen Strommarkt vergleichbar. Mögliche Neuanbieter auf dem Gasmarkt wären darauf angewiesen, das bestehende Leitungsnetz zu nutzen. Sie wären abhängig von den Konditionen für den Netzzugang. Damit können die Leitungseigner auf die Preise ihrer Konkurrenten Einfluss nehmen und deren Marktzugang erschweren.

3. Die Liberalisierungspolitik in Großbritannien und Deutschland im Vergleich

Dass die Liberalisierung ehemals staatseigener oder staatsnaher Wirtschaftssektoren auch anders gehen kann, lehrt das Ausland. Insbesondere die Liberalisierungspolitik Großbritanniens setzt Maßstäbe, sowohl in der Konzeption und Umsetzung der Liberalisierung als auch im Hinblick auf die Beteiligung der Verbraucherinteressen.

Konzeption und Umsetzung der Liberalisierungspolitik

In Großbritannien gibt die Regulierungsbehörde OFGEM seit Anfang der 90er Jahre den Unternehmen die Strom- und Gaspreise vor.[6] Außerdem wacht sie über die strikte rechtliche und wirtschaftliche Trennung von Kraftwerken und Übertragungsnetzen. Das verhindert Quersubventionen und fördert den Wettbewerb zwischen verschiedenen Anbietern, die das Netz nutzen. OFGEM folgt bei ihren Preisvorgaben für die 14 britischen Regionalgesellschaften einer einfachen Methode: Betriebe, die ihre Produktivität erhöhen können, müssen diesen Vorteil an ihre Kunden weitergeben, wobei allerdings die Inflationsrate und die Ausgaben für die Instandhaltung der Stromnetze und Gasleitungen sowie die Gelder für die Forschung angerechnet werden. Im Rhythmus von fünf Jahren werden die Preise angepasst.

Das britische System hat sich offensichtlich bewährt: Zumindest liegen die Preise in Großbritannien für die Industriekunden mit 5,42 Cent pro Kilowattstunde deutlich niedriger als in Deutschland (7,5 Cent).[7] Auch die Privathaushalte müssen in Großbritannien mit 8,4 Cent pro Kilowattstunde deutlich weniger zahlen als der deutsche Haushalt, dem 12,6 Cent (jeweils vor Steuern) abverlangt werden.[8]

---

6   Der Beitrag von Edward Blades (in diesem Band) bietet einen Überblick über das britische Modell der Regulierung des liberalisierten Strom- und Gasmarktes.
7   Zahlenangaben von Cerstin Gammelin, „Der deutsche Strom soll teuer bleiben", in „Die Zeit" vom 9.9.2004, S. 36.
8   Diese Preisangaben verdanke ich einer mündlichen Information von Edda Müller.

Aus Sicht der international vergleichenden politischen Ökonomie, ein Zweig der Sozialwissenschaften, ist diese – aus deutscher Perspektive „etatistische" – Liberalisierungspolitik Großbritanniens wenig überraschend. In der international vergleichenden Forschung gilt Großbritannien als eine „liberale Marktökonomie", im Unterschied zu den meisten anderen europäischen Ländern, die als „koordinierte Marktökonomien" bezeichnet werden (vgl. zum Beispiel Hall/ Soskice 2001). In Großbritannien gibt es ein großes Vertrauen in die Leistungskraft des Marktes, kombiniert mit einem eher restriktiven Staatsverständnis. Der Staat soll den Markt instand setzen, aber ansonsten auf Interventionen möglichst verzichten. Dieser Einordnung Großbritanniens als einer „liberalen Marktökonomie" entspricht, dass Großbritannien seine Netzsektoren früher und radikaler privatisiert und dereguliert hat als andere europäische Länder. Der Sachverhalt, dass Großbritannien eine handlungsfähige staatliche Regulierungsbehörde eingesetzt hat, um diese Liberalisierung voranzutreiben, widerspricht dem gängigen Bild Großbritanniens nicht. Die im europäischen Kontext einmalige „Westminster-Demokratie" gilt als recht entscheidungsfreudig und durchsetzungsstark, wenn es um die (staatlich abgesicherte) Stärkung der Marktkräfte geht.

Auch die bisherige Umsetzung der Liberalisierung in Deutschland ist aus Perspektive der international vergleichenden Sozialwissenschaft eine „typisch deutsche Geschichte." Es wird zwar auch in diesem Lande liberalisiert, aber die politische Vorgehensweise und das Umsetzungsmodell sehen völlig anders aus als in Großbritannien. Auf die Einsetzung einer Regulierungsbehörde hat die deutsche Politik bislang verzichtet. Stattdessen wurde ein völlig anderes Verfahren der Netzregelung gewählt: In sogenannten „Verbändevereinbarungen" haben die Unternehmen der Elektrizitätswirtschaft selbst die Bedingungen der Netznutzung aushandeln können. Bei dieser Konstruktion der Selbstregulierung handelt es sich um den erwiesenermaßen nicht immer glücklichen Versuch, die Regulierungsprobleme der Liberalisierung durch die Einberufung eines „runden Tisches" zu lösen, der eine allseits akzeptable Vereinbarung herbeiführen soll. Die Vereinbarung mit den Verbänden der Stromwirtschaft zur wettbewerbsgerechten Umsetzung der Liberalisierung des Strommarktes ist ein neues Beispiel für die in Deutschland gängige Praxis, bei öffentlichen Aufgaben die organisierten Interessen einzubinden (vgl. zur deutschen Vorliebe zu korporatistischen Arrangements Voelzkow 2000). Böse Zungen würden sagen, dass mit den Verbändevereinbarungen der Elektrizitätswirtschaft in der deutschen Variante der Liberalisierung der „Bock zum Gärtner gemacht" wurde.

Wenn hier die Verbändevereinbarungen bei der Liberalisierung der Elektrizitätswirtschaft als untauglicher Weg kritisiert werden, dann nicht, weil jedwedes korporatisisches Arrangement als unzulänglich eingestuft werden soll. Verbände können durchaus im Rahmen korporatistischer Arrangements staatsentlastend wirken, sofern ihre Verhandlungen unter dem „Schatten der Hierarchie" und damit unter dem Vorbehalt einer möglichen alternativen Regulierung durch den Staat stehen. Aber wenn dieser „Schatten der Hierarchie" zu schwach bleibt, sinkt auch das Entlastungspotential der Verbände, denn ihre Verhandlungsergebnisse schrumpfen auf den „kleinsten gemeinsamen Nenner" der beteiligten Verbände zusammen (vgl. dazu Voelzkow 1996). Bei der Liberalisierung der Energiewirtschaft war der „Schatten der Hierarchie" zwar spürbar, was die Elektrizitätswirtschaft auch zu gewissen Zugeständnissen gezwungen hat, wie sich insbesondere an den Nachbesserungen in der zweiten Verbändevereinbarung von 1999 zeigt (vgl. dazu näher Voß 2000). Aber der „Schatten der Hierarchie" war bislang letztlich zu schwach, um die nach wie vor bestehenden Defizite der deutschen Liberalisierungsvariante auszuräumen. Wenn es eine schlagkräftige Regulierungsbehörde mit Handlungsvollmachten und Drohpotential gäbe, dann würden vermutlich auch die korporatistischen Arrangements in der Liberalisierungspolitik besser greifen.

Bis heute aber leidet der deutsche Weg der Liberalisierung, wie Edda Müller (2004, S. 77ff.) kürzlich bilanziert hat, an „zwei Schönheitsfehlern". Der erste Schönheitsfehler besteht darin, dass die Trennung von Netz und Erzeugung („unbundling") nur formalrechtlich, aber nicht in Form einer Neuordnung der Eigentumsverhältnisse vorgenommen wurde. Dies ist ein folgenreicher Unterschied zu der Liberalisierungspolitik in anderen Ländern wie Großbritannien, den Niederlanden, Spanien oder Schweden, wo das „Unbundling" eine eigentumsrechtliche Trennung eingeschlossen hat. Der zweite Schönheitsfehler besteht darin, dass der deutsche Gesetzgeber die einzelnen konkreten Bedingungen und Regelungen zur Umsetzung der Liberalisierung den „betroffenen Wirtschaftskreisen" überlassen hat. Der Sachverhalt, dass die deutsche Liberalisierungspolitik nun in Reaktion auf die europäischen Richtlinien endlich doch eine Regulierungsbehörde einsetzen wird, ändert nichts an diesen beiden ins Auge stechenden „Schönheitsfehlern", solange die Regulierungsbehörde zu schwach bleibt. Einem zahnlosen Tiger kann die Energiewirtschaft gelassen entgegensehen.

Vertretung von Verbraucherinteressen

Was im deutsch-britischen Vergleich der Liberalisierungspolitik als eine Überraschung gewertet werden muss, die nicht so recht in das herkömmliche Bild des Landes passt, ist der Sachverhalt, dass die Privatisierung und Deregulierung der Netzsektoren in Großbritannien mit der institutionellen Verankerung einer organisierten Verbrauchervertretung verbunden wurde. Auf der Grundlage des „Utility Acts" sind in den verschiedenen „regulierten Märkten" spezielle Verbrauchereinrichtungen geschaffen worden. Dieses britische Modell der Watchdogs stützt sich auf sechs spezielle Organisationen, die zum Teil noch einen regional differenzierten Unterbau haben. Es handelt sich im Einzelnen um:

1. Energywatch[9]
2. Postwatch[10]
3. WaterVoice[11]
4. Financial Services Consumer Panel
5. OFCOM Consumer Panel
6. Air Transport Users Council

Hinter diesen sechs sektoralen Verbraucherorganisationen verbergen sich unterschiedliche Organisationsformen und Finanzierungsgrundlagen. Auch die Größenordnungen dieser organisierten Verbrauchervertretungen sind recht unterschiedlich. Aber in Großbritannien hat jeder liberalisierte Netzsektor seine eigene institutionalisierte Verbrauchervertretung bekommen.

Festzuhalten bleibt, dass Großbritannien die Erfahrung gemacht hat, dass die regulierten Märkte nicht von allein, das heißt nicht ohne weitere Regulierungsschritte funktionieren. Deshalb hat es in Großbritannien in den letzten Jahren nicht nur zahlreiche Reformen in der Liberalisierung der regulierten Märkte gegeben. Mitunter wurden ja sogar bereits vollzogene Schritte der Liberalisierung wieder zurückgenommen, weil sie sich nicht bewährt hatten (beispielsweise Privatisierung des Schienennetzes der Bahn). Um sicherzustellen, dass sich die Liberalisierung nicht gegen die Interessen der Verbraucher richtet, wurden als überraschende Innovation die *„Consumer Watchdogs"* eingerichtet. Sie sollen die Liberalisierungspolitik flankieren und unter kritischer Beobachtung halten.

Diese Politik entspricht nun eigentlich ganz und gar nicht dem Bild, das gemeinhin über Großbritannien gezeichnet wird. Eine solche staatlich ein- und angeleitete Organisation von Interessen, hier konkret die staatlich initiierte Organisation einer sektoralen Verbrauchervertretung in „regulierten Märkten", hat eher etwas von einem staatlich initiierten Korporatismus. So etwas ist in Großbritannien unüblich. Großbritannien wird in der international vergleichenden Verbandsforschung eher als ein pluralistisches System eingeordnet, das kaum korporatistische Arrange-

---

9   Zu den Aufgaben und der Organisation von Energywatch vgl. den Beitrag von Allan Asher (in diesem Band).
10 Vgl. den Beitrag von Gregor McGregor über „Postwatch" (in diesem Band).
11 Vgl. zu „WaterVoice" den Beitrag von Sheila Reiter (in diesem Band).

ments kennt. Die „*Consumer Watchdogs*" aber sind, wie schon allein ihre Entstehungsgeschichte und ihre Finanzierung deutlich machen, eine öffentliche Infrastruktur, die dafür sorgen soll, dass die Verbraucherinteressen in den liberalisierten Netzsektoren berücksichtigt werden.

Gleichwohl, auch in Großbritannien ist nicht alles Gold, was glänzt. Eine erste Bewertung der britischen Erfahrungen mit den „*Consumer Watchdogs*" ergibt einige kritische Befunde und Reformvorschläge, wie in einem Bericht des Department of Trade and Industry (DTI 2004) zu lesen ist. Ein Vorteil des britischen Modells liegt zweifelsohne darin, dass die Verbrauchervertretung institutionell und auch materiell abgesichert ist. Niemand käme heute in Großbritannien auf die Idee, die „*Watchdogs*" wieder ersatzlos abzuschaffen. Aber ein Nachteil des Modells ist darin zu sehen, dass es sich bei den „*Watchdogs*" eher um mehr oder minder effiziente „Beschwerdestellen" handelt, denen die Möglichkeit der direkten Einflussnahme und Mitbestimmung bei den Regulierungsbehörden noch fehlt.

Aber genau hier setzen auch die aktuellen Reformschläge an, die im Bericht des DTI (2004) enthalten sind. Vier Reformperspektiven stehen im Vordergrund:

(1) Die sektoralen Verbrauchereinrichtungen sollen in Zukunft nicht mehr nur Beschwerden der Verbraucher entgegennehmen und betreuen, sondern sie sollen in einem höheren Maße strategisch und pro-aktiv die Verbraucher gegenüber den Unternehmen und den Regulierungsbehörden sowie der Regierung repräsentieren.

(2) Die sektoralen Verbrauchereinrichtungen, die ja über die Kunden der Netzsektoren und über den Steuerzahler finanziert werden, sollen in Zukunft noch effizienter arbeiten. Rationalisierungspotentiale werden in dem Bericht in der regionalen Organisation und im Umgang mit den Beschwerden gesehen.

(3) Die Zusammenarbeit der sektoralen Verbrauchervertretung mit den Regulierungsbehörden, den Unternehmen und der Regierung soll verbessert werden, um sicherzustellen, dass die Verbraucherinteressen stärker in der Liberalisierungspolitik berücksichtigt werden.

(4) Um die Effizienz und die Effektivität der sektoralen Watchdogs zu verbessern, sollen sie untereinander besser kooperieren und eine gemeinsame Spitzenorganisation bilden, die sich in der Regulierung der Netzsektoren ein stärkeres Gehör verschaffen kann.

Wenn nun in Deutschland darüber nachgedacht wird, von den britischen Erfahrungen zu lernen und entsprechende Schlussfolgerungen auch im Hinblick auf die Vertretung der Verbraucherinteressen zu ziehen, dann sollten die Reformvorschläge in Großbritannien gleich mit einbezogen werden.

4. Zusammenfassung: Was kann Deutschland aus den britischen Erfahrungen lernen?

Die Liberalisierung von netzgebundenen Märkten ist und bleibt ein schwieriges Geschäft. Auch wenn im Grundsatz immer wieder unterstrichen wird, dass die Liberalisierung der regulierten Märkte im Interesse der Verbraucher erfolgen soll, ist keineswegs gesichert, dass die Liberalisierung dem Verbraucher auch tatsächlich Vorteile bringt. Zumindest besteht die Gefahr, dass private Monopole die ehemals öffentlichen Monopole ablösen und ihre Marktmacht missbrauchen. Der Verbraucher hätte dann nichts gewonnen. Deshalb ist es so ungemein wichtig, dass die Verbraucherinteressen über eine eigenständige Vertretung in die Liberalisierungspolitik eingespeist werden.

Die britischen Erfahrungen lehren, dass die Liberalisierung von regulierten Märkten mit einer institutionalisierten Verbrauchervertretung verknüpft werden kann. Es gehört zu den staatlichen Kernaufgaben der Liberalisierung, ein systematisches Qualitäts-Feedback-System für die Bürger oder die Verbraucher in die liberalisierten Märkte einzubauen, das möglichst unabhängig von der Regierung und den Regulierungsbehörden arbeitet. Die britischen *„Watchdogs"* sind ein bewährtes Beispiel aus der Praxis, wie ein solches systematisches Kunden- oder Bürger-Qualitäts-Feedback-System aussehen kann. Die britischen „Consumer Watchdogs" sind ein Weg, die verstärkte Nutzung der (staatlich regulierten) Marktkoordination mit einer institutionellen Stärkung des Verbraucherschutzes zu kombinieren. Damit sind die britischen *„Watchdogs"* ein „Best-Practice-Modell" öffentlicher Aufgabenerfüllung in regulierten Märkten. Im Grundsatz wollen die Verbraucher eine Ergebnissteuerung – statt einer administrativen Regelsetzung. Aber Ergebnissteuerung setzt entsprechende Informations- und Rückkopplungssysteme sowie eine Vertretung der Verbraucherinteressen (wie die *„Watchdogs"*) voraus.

Was hier in Deutschland zur selbstkritischen Diskussion Anlass geben sollte, ist der überraschende Sachverhalt, dass ausgerechnet das liberale Großbritannien, das gemeinhin wie kein anderes Land auf den Markt setzt, den Aufbau eines differenzierten Qualitäts-Feedback-Systems für Kunden und Bürger zum Bestandteil seiner Liberalisierungspolitik gemacht hat. An diese praktischen Erfahrungen in Großbritannien könnte die deutsche Verbraucherpolitik anknüpfen.

In Deutschland gibt es bereits eine organisierte Interessenvertretung der Verbraucher. Mit dem Verbraucherzentrale Bundesverband e.V. ist eine handlungsfähige Spitzenorganisation der Verbraucher verfügbar. Aber dem Verbraucherzentrale Bundesverband fehlt bis heute das öffentliche Mandat (also rechtlich abgesicherte Anhörungs- und Beteiligungsrechte und sowie eine an diese Aufgabe gekoppelte Finanzierungsgrundlage), um die Regulierung der Netzsektoren kritisch begleiten und die Liberalisierungspolitik im Interesse des Verbrauchers (auch gegenüber der zukünftigen Regulierungsbehörde) beeinflussen zu können.

Literatur:

DTI (Department of Trade and Industry and HM Treasury) 2004: Consumer Representation in regulated Markets. Final Report.

Hall, Peter/ Soskice, David (eds.) 2001: Varieties of Capitalism. The Institutional Foundations of Comparative Advantage. Oxford: Oxford University Press.

Hughes, Thomas P. 1983: Networks of Power. Electrification 1880 – 1930. Baltimore, MD: John Hopkins University Press.

Knieps, Günther 2004: Der Wettbewerb und seine Grenzen: Netzgebundene Leistungen aus ökonomischer Sicht. In: vzbv 2004, S. 11-26.

Voelzkow, Helmut 1996: Private Regierungen in der Techniksteuerung. Eine sozialwissenschaftliche Analyse der technischen Normung. Frankfurt am Main: Campus.

Voelzkow, Helmut 2000: Korporatismus in Deutschland: Chancen, Risiken und Perspektiven. In: Everhard Holtmann/Helmut Voelzkow (Hrsg.) 2000: Zwischen Wettbewerbs- und Verhandlungsdemokratie. Analysen zum Regierungssystem der Bundesrepublik Deutschland. Wiesbaden: Westdeutscher Verlag, S. 185-212.

Voß, Jan-Peter 2000: Institutionelle Arrangements zwischen Zukunfts- und Gegenwartsfähigkeit: Netzregulierung im liberalisierten deutschen Stromsektor. In: Volker von Prittwitz (Hrsg.), Institutionelle Arrangements in der Umweltpolitik. Opladen: Leske + Budrich, S. 227-254.

vzbv (Verbraucherzentrale Bundesverband e.V.) 2004: Verbraucherschutz in netzgebundenen Märkten. Wie viel Staat braucht der Markt? Dokumentation der Tagung vom 18. November 2003. Berlin: Verbraucherzentrale Bundesverband e.V.

IV. Wettbewerbsprobleme im Strommarkt: die Sicht der Monopolkommission

Sabine Streb

Die Monopolkommission beschäftigt sich seit vielen Jahren mit der Wettbewerbsentwicklung in der deutschen Elektrizitätswirtschaft. In ihrem im Jahr 2002 veröffentlichten 14. Hauptgutachten hat sie die grundsätzliche Problematik der Regulierung von Netzsektoren aufgegriffen. Sie ist dabei auch auf die Netzzugangsproblematik im Elektrizitätssektor eingegangen und hat auf die Schwierigkeiten hingewiesen, die sich bei der Durchsetzung des Netzzugangsanspruchs von Wettbewerbern auf der Grundlage des „verhandelten Netzzugangs" in Verbindung mit der Ex-post-Missbrauchsaufsicht durch das Bundeskartellamt ergeben. Bereits zum damaligen Zeitpunkt hat die Monopolkommission die Befürchtung geäußert, der Wettbewerb im Elektrizitätssektor könne zum Stillstand kommen. Zu dieser Einschätzung gelangte sie aufgrund der marktstrukturellen Entwicklungen sowie der unzulänglichen Ausgestaltung des elektrizitätswirtschaftlichen Regulierungsrahmens. Durch die seither eingetretene Marktentwicklung sieht sich die Monopolkommission leider ebenso in ihrer damaligen Einschätzung bestätigt wie durch die Erfahrungen des Bundeskartellamtes, missbräuchlich überhöhte Netzentgelte mit den Instrumenten des allgemeinen Wettbewerbrechts in den Griff zu bekommen.

Die Monopolkommission hat die mittlerweile in aller Deutlichkeit zu Tage getretenen wettbewerblichen Fehlentwicklungen auf den deutschen Strommärkten in ihrem 15. Hauptgutachten einer umfassenden Würdigung unterzogen. Im Ergebnis ist sie dabei zu der Auffassung gelangt, dass die wettbewerbliche Dynamik der Anfangsphase nach der Liberalisierung der Strommärkte deutlich nachgelassen hat und ein nahezu wettbewerbsloser Zustand eingetreten ist. Nach Ansicht der Monopolkommission sind die Ursachen für diese Entwicklung sowohl in der Verschlechterung der marktstrukturellen Bedingungen für Wettbewerb in der Elektrizitätswirtschaft als auch in Wettbewerbsbehinderungen durch monopolistisch überhöhte Netzentgelte zu suchen.

1. Markt- und Wettbewerbsentwicklung

Die Struktur der Märkte in der deutschen Elektrizitätswirtschaft hat sich innerhalb weniger Jahre durch die unmittelbar nach der Marktöffnung einsetzenden intensiven Fusionsaktivitäten grundlegend verändert. Dabei haben sowohl horizontale als auch vertikale Zusammenschlüsse die Anzahl der Energieversorgungsunternehmen reduziert und die Konzentration im Stromsektor beträchtlich erhöht. Auf der Verbundebene haben horizontale Zusammenschlüsse zur Herausbildung eines marktbeherrschenden, wettbewerbslosen Oligopols, bestehend aus E.ON Energie, RWE, Vattenfall Europe und EnBW AG, geführt. Diese vier Unternehmen verfügen nicht nur vollständig über das Stromübertragungsnetz, sondern auch über circa 80 Prozent der Stromerzeugungskapazitäten in Deutschland. Darüber hinaus sind sie in großem Umfang direkt oder über Tochtergesellschaften in der Endkundenversorgung tätig. Die vertikale Integration war in Deutschland schon vor der Marktöffnung sehr ausgeprägt. Sie schreitet durch die zahlreichen Beteiligungen der vier Verbundunternehmen beziehungsweise ihrer regionalen Tochtergesellschaften an kommunalen Energieversorgungsunternehmen weiter voran. Mit diesen Beteiligungen sind erhebliche wettbewerbsbeschränkende Wirkungen verbunden, da die Verbundunternehmen einen beträchtlichen Einfluss auf das Beschaffungsverhalten der örtlichen Energieversorger erhalten. Sie sichern dadurch langfristig ihren Stromabsatz. Dies ist auch dann der Fall, wenn es sich „nur" um Minderheitsbeteiligungen von zehn oder 20 Prozent handelt. Potentielle Wettbewerber werden von einem Marktzutritt abgeschreckt und die Strommärkte auf diese Weise weiter abgeschottet. Nach den Ermittlungen des Bundeskartellamtes halten die vier Verbundunternehmen gegenwärtig an über 300 Regionalversorgern und Stadtwerken Mehrheits- und Minderheitsbeteiligungen.

Wettbewerbspolitisch von Bedeutung ist ferner die von den Verbundunternehmen und ihren Tochtergesellschaften betriebene Integration von Strom- und Gasversorgungsunternehmen. Das bedeutendste Ereignis in diesem Zusammenhang war die durch Ministererlaubnis freigegebene Fusion zwischen E.ON und Ruhrgas. Durch ihre Beteiligungen an Gasimportgesellschaften und regionalen Gasweiterverteilern erhalten die Verbundunternehmen einen großen Einfluss auf die Höhe des Gaspreises. Für die Strommärkte ist dies insofern relevant, als Erdgas in Zukunft eine zunehmend wichtigere Rolle in der Stromerzeugung spielen wird. Die Hoffnungen auf eine Belebung des Wettbewerbs durch neue Marktteilnehmer aus dem In- und Ausland haben sich nicht erfüllt. Vielmehr konnten viele der unmittelbar nach der Marktöffnung neu in den deutschen Markt eingetretenen Anbieter ihre Marktposition nicht festigen und sind mittlerweile wieder aus dem Markt ausgeschieden. So haben mehrere der in den Markt eingetretenen ausländischen Anbieter ihre Beteiligungen an deutschen Energieversorgungsunternehmen bereits wieder verkauft beziehungsweise ihre Handelsaktivitäten aufgrund ungenügender Geschäftsaussichten aufgegeben. Auf dem Markt für die Belieferung von Kleinkunden sind viele der neu gegründeten Unternehmen zahlungsunfähig und haben ihre Geschäftstätigkeit eingestellt. Insgesamt hat sich die Zahl der Wettbewerber inzwischen deutlich reduziert. Eine Belebung des Wettbewerbs könnte angesichts der hohen Konzentration auf der Erzeugerebene in Deutschland am ehesten durch Importe ausländischer Anbieter erfolgen. Dem stehen allerdings die begrenzten Netzkapazitäten an den Kuppelstellen ins Ausland entgegen.

Die nachlassende Intensität des Wettbewerbs zeigt sich nach Auffassung der Monopolkommission in dem Aufwärtstrend bei den Strompreisen. Nachdem die Strompreise unmittelbar nach der Marktöffnung sowohl für Industrie- als auch für Haushaltskunden deutlich gesunken sind, beginnen sie seit dem Jahr 2000 für alle Verbrauchergruppen wieder zu steigen. Nach Schätzung des Verbandes der Elektrizitätswirtschaft haben die Strompreise für Haushaltskunden bereits wieder das Niveau vor der Marktöffnung erreicht. Für Industriekunden liegen die Nettostrompreise nach den Erhebungen von Eurostat europaweit an der Spitze. Die aktuell angekündigten Strompreiserhöhungen durch die vier Verbundunternehmen bestätigen diesen nun schon seit geraumer Zeit zu beobachtenden Trend. Der Anstieg der Endverbraucherpreise ist dabei nicht, wie verschiedentlich vorgebracht, allein auf die zusätzlichen Belastungen aus der Ökosteuer, dem Erneuerbare-Energien-Gesetz oder dem Kraft-Wärme-Kopplungsgesetz zurückzuführen. Er geht vielmehr zu einem beträchtlichen Teil auch auf die steigenden Erzeugerpreise zurück, wie unter anderem durch die Kursentwicklung des Spotmarktes an der Leipziger Strombörse belegt wird. Einen weiteren Indikator für die geringe Wettbewerbsintensität auf den deutschen Strommärkten stellt die beispielsweise im Vergleich mit Großbritannien sehr niedrige Wechselrate bei den Haushalts- und Gewerbekunden dar. So haben nur circa fünf Prozent der Haushalts- und Gewerbekunden bis zum Herbst 2002 ihren Stromversorger gewechselt. Der von dieser Kundengruppe ausgehende Wettbewerbsdruck ist nach Auffassung der Monopolkommission daher als eher gering einzustufen.

Zusammenfassend stellt sich nach Ansicht der Monopolkommission die Wettbewerbsentwicklung in der deutschen Elektrizitätswirtschaft seit der Liberalisierung wie folgt dar: Mit der im Jahr 1998 erfolgten Marktöffnung erhielten Endverbraucher die Möglichkeit, ihren Stromanbieter selbst zu wählen. Von dieser Möglichkeit machten zunächst industrielle Großkunden und weiterverteilende lokale Versorgungsunternehmen Gebrauch, die sich aus ihren langfristigen Bezugsverträgen lösten. Nach der Verabschiedung der Verbändevereinbarung II und der Einführung von Standardlastprofilen für Haushaltskunden führte unter anderem auch der Marktzutritt bundesweit agierender Handelstöchter der Verbundunternehmen zu einem intensiveren Wettbewerb um Haushaltskunden. Der zunehmende Wettbewerbsdruck hatte zu günstigeren Preisen für industrielle Großkunden, lokale Verteilunternehmen und auch für Haushaltskunden geführt. Die Wettbewerbsdynamik der Anfangsphase nach der Liberalisierung war jedoch nur von kurzer Dauer. Der Preiswettbewerb zwischen den Verbundunternehmen stellte sich als Übergangsphänomen heraus, mit dem der drohende Marktzutritt neuer Anbieter abgewehrt und ein Abwandern der Stadtwerke zu neuen Lieferanten verhindert werden sollte. Die schwache Wettbewerbsdynamik erklärt sich außerdem aus den bei der Liberalisierung vorhandenen Überkapazitäten im Erzeugungsbereich. Der von den Verbundunternehmen seit 2001 betriebene Abbau von Erzeugungskapazitäten und der gleichzeitig zu beobachtende Wiederanstieg der Strompreise lässt jedoch darauf schließen, dass die Phase kurzfristigen Preiswettbewerbs zwischen den Verbundunternehmen beendet und einem abgestimmten Verhalten der Oligopolmitglieder gewichen ist. Diese beschränken sich darauf, ihre traditionellen Absatzgebiete zu beliefern und verzichten auf Wettbewerbsvorstöße in das Liefergebiet der jeweils anderen Verbundunternehmen. Wie Marktteilnehmer berichten, haben es mittlerweile selbst industrielle Großkunden schwer, wettbewerbliche Angebote zu erhalten. Ein durchgreifender Lieferantenwechsel hat weder bei Großabnehmern noch bei Haushaltskunden stattgefunden. Vielmehr werden beispielsweise fast alle Stadtwerke von ihrem ehemaligen Vorlieferanten beliefert. Nach Auffassung der Monopolkommission ähneln die heutigen Marktstrukturen in der deutschen Elektrizitätswirtschaft weitgehend den rechtlich abgeschotteten Gebietsmonopolen vor der Liberalisierung.

2. Wettbewerbsprobleme beim Netzzugang

Die derzeitigen Marktstrukturen geben also wenig Anlass für eine optimistische Prognose hinsichtlich der zukünftigen Wettbewerbsentwicklung in der deutschen Elektrizitätswirtschaft. Das Bild trübt sich weiter, wenn man den gesetzlichen Regulierungsrahmen betrachtet, welcher der wettbewerbspolitischen Problematik und der wirtschaftlichen Bedeutung des Stromsektors wenig angemessen ist.

Stromübertragungs- und -verteilnetze stellen, wie wir Ökonomen dies nennen, natürliche Monopole dar. Dies bedeutet, dass der Aufbau paralleler Leitungssysteme aus Kostengründen in der Regel nicht wirtschaftlich ist. Wettbewerb in der Stromübertragung und in der Stromverteilung ist daher in der Regel ausgeschlossen. In der Stromerzeugung und im Stromhandel ist Wettbewerb dagegen durchaus möglich. Eine notwendige Voraussetzung für die wettbewerbliche Betätigung Dritter in der Stromerzeugung und im Stromhandel ist allerdings der Zugang zu den Leitungssystemen der monopolistischen Netzbetreiber. Als natürliche Monopole stellen die Stromnetze die Wettbewerbspolitik aber vor besondere Aufgaben. Zum einen haben monopolistische Netzbetreiber keinen Anreiz, ihre Dienstleistung zu einem wettbewerbsanalogen Preis bereitzustellen. Es ist vielmehr davon auszugehen, dass durch missbräuchlich überhöhte Netzentgelte Monopolgewinne aus dem Netzbetrieb realisiert werden. Zum zweiten haben monopolistische Stromnetzbetreiber, die selbst auf den Stromerzeugungs- und -einzelhandelsmärkten tätig sind, beträchtliche Anreize, ihre Wettbewerber, die auf die Nutzung des Netzes angewiesen sind, zu behindern. Dies kann durch eine diskriminierende Ausgestaltung der Netzzugangsbedingungen oder durch überhöhte Netzpreise geschehen. Der Betrieb von Stromnetzen ist insofern grundsätzlich einer speziellen Wettbewerbs- oder Regulierungsaufsicht zu unterstellen. Dies gilt im Übrigen auch dann, wenn die Anreize für eine Diskriminierung von Wettbewerbern durch eine eigentumsrechtliche Trennung der Netze von den übrigen stromwirtschaftlichen Aktivitäten beseitigt würden. Das Problem missbräuchlich überhöhter Netzentgelte zur Erzielung von Monopolrenten wäre damit ja nicht beseitigt.

In Deutschland hat man im Gegensatz zu allen anderen europäischen Ländern zum Zeitpunkt der Marktöffnung auf eine explizite regulierende Kontrolle der Netzzugangsmodalitäten und der Netzentgelte durch eine sektorspezifische Regulierungsbehörde verzichtet. Man hatte gehofft, die Funktionsfähigkeit des Wettbewerbs in der Energiewirtschaft auf dem Wege des „verhandelten Netzzugangs" sicherstellen zu können. Die Ausgestaltung des Netzzugangs sollte ebenso wie die Festlegung der Netzentgelte den Marktteilnehmern überlassen bleiben. Der Missbrauchsaufsicht durch das Bundeskartellamt kam in diesem Modell die entscheidende Rolle für die Durchsetzung des Netzzugangsanspruches zu.

Die Hoffnung, mittels Selbstregulierung und den Kontrollinstrumenten des allgemeinen Wettbewerbsrechts funktionsfähigen Wettbewerb in der Elektrizitätswirtschaft sicherstellen zu können, hat sich nach Auffassung der Monopolkommission jedoch als Illusion erwiesen. Die elektrizitätswirtschaftlich einschlägigen Verbände haben sich in den mehrfach modifizierten Verbändevereinbarungen über die Rahmenbedingungen für den Netzzugang und die Kalkulation der Netzentgelte geeinigt. Allerdings belassen die in der aktuellen Version der Verbändevereinbarung, der Verbändevereinbarung Strom II plus, niedergelegten Preiskalkulationsprinzipien den Netzbetreibern erhebliche Spielräume bei der Festlegung der Netzpreise. Dies wird durch die überaus große Bandbreite der Netzentgelte in Deutschland belegt. Die Kalkulationsprinzipien der Verbändevereinbarung bieten also keine Gewähr dafür, dass die nach ihnen kalkulierten Netzentgelte nicht missbräuchlich sind. Das auch im internationalen Vergleich überdurchschnittlich hohe Niveau der Netzentgelte erweist sich derzeit als das zentrale Wettbewerbshindernis in der deutschen Stromwirtschaft. Nach Ansicht der Monopolkommission lässt sich das Problem monopolistisch überhöhter Netzpreise mit der Verbändevereinbarung

Strom II plus nicht in den Griff bekommen. Eine Kontrolle missbräuchlich überhöhter Netzentgelte ist im Modell des verhandelten Netzzugangs allenfalls von der Missbrauchsaufsicht des Bundeskartellamtes zu erwarten. Die Erfahrungen, die das Bundeskartellamt in den letzten beiden Jahren mit der Missbrauchsaufsicht über monopolistische Netzbetreiber gemacht hat, haben allerdings die Begrenztheit des kartellrechtlichen Instrumentariums zur Kontrolle missbräuchlich überhöhter Netzentgelte in aller Deutlichkeit vor Augen geführt.

Das Bundeskartellamt hat im Frühjahr 2003 erstmals zwei Verfügungen aufgrund missbräuchlich überhöhter Netzentgelte erlassen. Dabei hat es eine Obergrenze für die Gesamterlöse aus dem Netzbetrieb festgelegt, die von den betroffenen Unternehmen, der Thüringer Energie AG und den Stadtwerken Mainz, nicht überschritten werden darf. Beide Unternehmen hatten beim Oberlandesgericht Düsseldorf Beschwerde gegen die Missbrauchsverfügung des Bundeskartellamtes eingelegt. Die Beschwerde hat in beiden Fällen zur Aufhebung der Missbrauchsverfügung des Bundeskartellamtes geführt. Begründet hat das Gericht seine Entscheidung unter anderem damit, dass die beiden Netzbetreiber ihre Netzentgelte in Übereinstimmung mit den Kalkulationsprinzipien der Verbändevereinbarung Strom II plus festgelegt hätten. Es ist nach Auffassung des Gerichts daher davon auszugehen, dass der Vermutungstatbestand „guter fachlicher Praxis", den der Gesetzgeber bei der letzten Novelle des Energiewirtschaftsgesetzes eingeführt hat, erfüllt ist. Wie schon erwähnt, garantieren die Kalkulationsprinzipien der Verbändevereinbarung Strom II plus jedoch keineswegs die Missbrauchsfreiheit der nach ihnen kalkulierten Netzentgelte. Das Gericht hat außerdem die Festlegung einer Erlösobergrenze für nicht zulässig erklärt, da die Festsetzung einer derartigen Obergrenze auf eine kartellrechtlich nicht gedeckte präventive Preiskontrolle hinauslaufe. Außerdem dürfe sich das Bundeskartellamt nicht ausschließlich auf eine Überprüfung der Gesamterlöse beschränken, sondern müsse zusätzlich eine Überprüfung der Einzelpreise vornehmen.

Nach Ansicht der Monopolkommission verdeutlichen die Entscheidungen des Oberlandesgerichts die erheblichen Schwächen der Ex-post-Missbrauchsaufsicht über die Netzentgelte in der Stromwirtschaft. Diese bestehen vor allem darin, dass das Bundeskartellamt die Beweislast für die Angemessenheit der Netzentgelte trägt. Wie die Gerichtsentscheidungen zu diesen und früheren Fällen sowie auch außerhalb der Stromwirtschaft zeigen, kann das Bundeskartellamt den Beweisanforderungen der Gerichte in Preismissbrauchsfällen in aller Regel nicht Genüge tun. Die Vorschriften des Gesetzes gegen Wettbewerbsbeschränkungen zur Preishöhenkontrolle bei marktbeherrschenden Unternehmen sind durch die Rechtsprechung bisher weitgehend ins Leere gelaufen.

Hinter der Beweisproblematik steht ein tiefergehendes konzeptionelles Problem der Preisaufsicht über monopolistische Stromnetzbetreiber. Dieses besteht zum einen darin, dass keine wettbewerblichen Vergleichsmaßstäbe zur Beurteilung der Angemessenheit von Netzentgelten zur Verfügung stehen. Die Netzentgelte anderer Netzbetreiber, die beim Vergleichsmarktkonzept als Maßstab für die Missbräuchlichkeit herangezogen werden, stellen nämlich ebenfalls nur mangelhaft wettbewerblich beeinflusste Monopolpreise dar. In der Regel wird eine Aufsichtsbehörde daher immer gezwungen sein, Einblick in die Kostensituation der Netzbetreiber zu nehmen. Selbst bei einem vollständigen Einblick in die Kostensituation kann die Aufsichtsbehörde aber nur begrenzt beurteilen, inwieweit die nachgewiesenen Kosten unter Effizienzgesichtspunkten gerechtfertigt sind und der Netzbetreiber bestehende Rationalisierungspotentiale ausgeschöpft hat. Die Aufsichtsbehörde steht damit vor einem grundsätzlichen Informationsproblem. Dieses Informationsproblem führt dazu, dass bei einer ausschließlich kostenbasierten Überprüfung der Netzentgelte der Netzbetreiber keine Anreize hat, durch effizienzerhöhende Maßnahmen seine Kosten zu senken. Höhere Kosten können als betriebsnotwendig dargestellt und über höhere Preise auf die Netznutzer abgewälzt werden. Bei der Überprüfung von Netzentgelten besteht ein weiteres konzeptionelles Problem für die Aufsichtsbehörde darin, die Angemessenheit der Zuordnung von Fix- und Gemeinkosten auf den Netzbetrieb beziehungsweise die einzelnen Netzdienstleistungen überprüfen zu müssen. Für den vertikal integrierten Netzbetreiber bestehen aber erhebliche Anreize, möglichst viele Kosten dem Netzbetrieb zuzuordnen. Die Zuordnung von Fix- und Gemeinkosten auf den Netzbetrieb beziehungsweise auf die einzelnen Netzdienstleistungen ist ein komplexes Problem, für das es in der ökonomischen Theorie keine einfachen, allgemein gültigen Regeln gibt. Vielmehr wurden verschiedene Zuordnungsregeln und Regulierungsverfahren entwickelt, die jeweils spezifische Vor- und Nachteile aufweisen. Sie unterscheiden sich im Hinblick auf ihre Effizienzeigenschaften, ihre Praktikabilität, die Informationsanforderungen, die sie an die Regulierungsbehörde stellen und im Hinblick auf die Preissetzungsspielräume, die sie dem Netzbetreiber bei der Festlegung von Einzelpreisen belassen. Ich möchte hier nicht im Einzelnen auf die Vor- und Nachteile verschiedener Kostenzurechungs- und Regulierungsverfahren eingehen. Weil es keine einfachen, eindeutigen Zuordnungsregeln gibt, bleibt jedoch weitgehend unklar, anhand welcher Kriterien eine Aufsichtsbehörde den Gerichten im Einzelfall einen Preismissbrauch nachweisen kann, falls sich die gerichtliche Entscheidung auch auf die materielle Überprüfung von Einzelpreisen erstreckt.

Vor diesem Hintergrund hat die Monopolkommission schon im 14. Hauptgutachten vor zwei Jahren die Einführung einer Ex-ante-Preisregulierung (nach dem Vorbild beispielsweise des Vereinigten Königreiches) für die Netzpreise in der Stromwirtschaft empfohlen. Die seither eingetretenen Entwicklungen haben sie darin noch bestärkt. Eine Ex-ante-Regulierung der Netzentgelte hätte nach Ansicht der Monopolkommission verschiedene Vorteile. Zum einen wäre das Problem der Beweislast kleiner, wenn dem Regulierer von vornherein die Kompetenz zur Festsetzung der Netzpreise gegeben würde. Darüber hinaus wäre es dem Regulierer möglich, anreizorientierte Regulierungsverfahren zu entwickeln und anzuwenden. Dass mit anreizorientierten Regulierungsverfahren erhebliche Effizienzverbesserungen erreicht werden können, wird durch internationale Erfahrungen, beispielsweise in Großbritannien, belegt. Schließlich wäre die Aufsichtsbehörde bei einer Ex-ante-Regulierung in der Lage, komplexe Verfahrensstrukturen zu entwickeln, die dem Problem der Zurechnung von Fix- und Gemeinkosten Rechnung tragen. Nach den Vorstellungen der Monopolkommission sollte der Regulierungsbehörde die Wahl eines Preisregulierungsverfahrens innerhalb bestimmter gesetzlicher Rahmenbedingungen grundsätzlich freigestellt sein. Für die Regulierung der Netzpreise schlägt die Monopolkommission ein zweistufiges Verfahren vor. Die Regulierungsbehörde hätte auf einer ersten Stufe Verfahrensgrundsätze zu entwickeln, die regeln, welches Preisregulierungsmodell anzuwenden ist. In einem zweiten Schritt würde sie auf der Grundlage dieser Grundsätze die einzelnen Netzentgelte genehmigen. Ein solches System hätte den Vorteil, dass sich die gerichtliche Überprüfung der Regulierungsentscheidungen darauf beschränken würde, ob die von der Regulierungsbehörde entwickelten Verfahrensgrundsätze mit den übergeordneten gesetzlichen Normen übereinstimmen und darauf, ob die genehmigten Einzelpreise mit den Verfahrensgrundsätzen der Regulierungsbehörde konsistent sind. Die materiellrechtliche Überprüfung der „Angemessenheit" von Einzelentgelten durch Gerichte entfiele. Im Gegensatz dazu kann bei Ex-post-Missbrauchsverfahren eine gerichtliche Prüfung von Einzelpreisen nicht vermieden werden.

3. Beurteilung des vorgelegten Gesetzentwurfs für ein novelliertes Energiewirtschaftsgesetz

Vor dem Hintergrund dieser Überlegungen dürfte deutlich geworden sein, dass die Monopolkommission in dem vorliegenden Regierungsentwurf für die Novellierung des Energiewirtschaftsgesetzes keine substanzielle Verbesserung der regulatorischen Rahmenbedingungen für den Elektrizitätssektor erkennen kann. Dies gilt insbesondere im Hinblick auf das vorgesehene System der Netzentgeltregulierung. Der vorgelegte Gesetzentwurf weist die folgenden grundlegenden Schwächen auf, die eine wirksame und effektive Kontrolle monopolistisch überhöhter Netzentgelte nach Ansicht der Monopolkommission nicht erwarten lassen:

1. Die Regulierungsbehörde erhält keine Kompetenzen für eine Ex-ante-Genehmigung der Netzentgelte. Ex ante genehmigt werden sollen lediglich die Bedingungen und Methoden für den Netzzugang. Die Netzentgelte unterliegen weiterhin nur einer Ex-post-Missbrauchskontrolle durch die Regulierungsbehörde, die sich dadurch bei der gerichtlichen Überprüfung von Regulierungsentscheidungen denselben Beweislastproblemen gegenüber sieht, an denen schon das Bundeskartellamt gescheitert ist.

2. Der Gesetzentwurf räumt dem Bundeswirtschaftsministerium an zentralen Stellen umfangreiche Befugnisse zum Erlass von Rechtsverordnungen ein. Die vorliegenden ersten Entwürfe einer Netzzugangs- und Netzentgeltverordnung Strom lassen eine weitgehende verordnungsrechtliche Normierung von Kostenkalkulationsprinzipien erwarten. Als Grundlage werden dabei die Preisfindungskriterien der Verbändevereinbarung Strom II plus herangezogen. Hierdurch werden die Handlungsspielräume der zukünftigen Regulierungsbehörde deutlich verringert. Es ist zu befürchten, dass sich die Kompetenzen der Regulierungsbehörde im Bereich der Marktregulierung auf eine rein formale Überprüfung verordnungsrechtlich vorgegebener Kalkulationsprinzipien beschränken werden. Dies ist den ökonomischen Problemen der Netzentgeltregulierung nicht angemessen. Die Entwicklung ökonomisch und wettbewerblich sachgerechter Preisregulierungsverfahren benötigt erfahrungsgemäß Zeit. Voraussetzung für eine effiziente Regulierung der Netzpreise ist daher ein Regulierungsrahmen, der es der Regulierungsbehörde ermöglicht, Erfahrungen zu sammeln und die Entgeltregulierung im Sinne eines Lernprozesses in flexibler Weise an dynamische Marktentwicklungen anzupassen.

3. Der vorliegende Gesetzentwurf stellt weitgehend auf eine kostenorientierte Prüfung der Netzentgelte ab. Für die Einführung anreizorientierter Regulierungsinstrumente enthält der Entwurf keine Ermächtigungsgrundlage. Das vorgesehene Vergleichsverfahren, um den die kostenorientierte Regulierung der Netzentgelte ergänzt werden soll, stellt kein anreizorientiertes, auf Effizienzverbesserungen abzielendes Regulierungsinstrument dar. Sofern das Vergleichsverfahren auf einen Vergleich von Netzentgelten beispielsweise Netzerlösen abstellt, ist dies schon konzeptionell mit dem Problem verbunden, dass als Vergleichsmaßstab die möglicherweise ebenfalls monopolistisch überhöhten Entgelte und Erlöse des Vergleichsunternehmens herangezogen werden. Durch einen Vergleich von Monopolpreisen ist aber ein insgesamt überhöhtes Niveau der Netzentgelte nicht nachzuweisen. Auch ein Kostenvergleich kann nur dann Anreizwirkungen für zukünftige Effizienzverbesserungen entfalten, wenn seine Ergebnisse in die Festlegung von Preisobergrenzen im Rahmen einer Ex-ante-

Regulierung einfließen. Dabei erhalten dann relativ kosteneffiziente Netzbetreiber großzügigere Preisvorgaben als Netzbetreiber mit überdurchschnittlich hohen Kosten. Auf diese Weise ließe sich ein gewisser Wettbewerb zwischen den Netzbetreibern simulieren, der Anreize für Effizienzverbesserungen bei allen Netzbetreibern setzt.

Die Monopolkommission hofft, dass der vorliegende Regierungsentwurf im weiteren Verlauf des Gesetzgebungsprozesses noch entsprechend modifiziert und ein Rechtsrahmen für die Entwicklung einer anreizorientierten Ex-ante-Regulierung geschaffen wird. Bleibt es dagegen bei dem bisher vorgesehenen System der kostenbasierten Entgeltregulierung in Verbindung mit der nachträglichen Kontrolle der Netzpreise, steht zu befürchten, dass die wettbewerbliche Entwicklung der Strommärkte weiterhin stagnieren wird und die Endverbraucher auch in Zukunft mit steigenden Strompreisen rechnen müssen.

V. Regulierung des Strom- und Gasmarktes und Verbraucherinteressen

Alois Rhiel

Energiepolitik und Energiepreise sind von herausragender Bedeutung für die Industrie wie auch für die Kaufkraft der Privathaushalte. Nicht nur bei der Konzeption der neuen Regulierung lohnt es sich, die guten Erfahrungen im Ausland sowie auf anderen Infrastrukturmärkten zu nutzen. Auch für die Praxis können wir lernen. Dabei unterstütze ich den Vorschlag des Bundesverbands der Verbraucherzentralen, die Anliegen der Verbraucher bei der künftigen Regulierung im Energiemarkt stärker zu beachten. Die Erfahrungen aus Großbritannien legen es nahe, zu überlegen, ob es auch in Deutschland für Haushalte und Unternehmen vorteilhaft wäre, wenn eine besondere Interessenvertretung für Verbraucher der Regulierungsbehörde angegliedert würde. Die Regulierung wird nur dann wirkungsvoll funktionieren, wenn für das Management von Beschwerden der Energieverbraucher effiziente Strukturen innerhalb der Regulierungsbehörde vorhanden sind. Die negativen Erfahrungen von Haushalten in Deutschland, denen Energieversorger einen Wechsel zu günstigeren Stromanbietern erschwert haben oder unmöglich machten, mahnen uns, dass wir nun ausreichend Vorsorge gegen solche Wettbewerbsbeschränkungen treffen. Besonders die Bundesregierung offenbart noch einen großen Nachholbedarf in Wettbewerbspolitik.

Die Politik soll dabei jedoch nur in das Marktsegment regulierend eingreifen, wo der Wettbewerb aus marktstrukturellen Gründen versagt. Wo hingegen Wettbewerb möglich ist, muss sich der Staat raushalten oder die Regulierung abbauen. Für den Energiemarkt in Deutschland heißt das, dass bei Erzeugung und Verkauf von Strom wettbewerbspolitisch keine Regulierung nötig ist, weil in diesen Marktsegmenten der Wettbewerb funktionieren kann. Hingegen gibt es auf den Märkten für die Energiedurchleitung unbestreitbare natürliche Monopole. Hier herrscht Wettbewerbsversagen. Hier muss der Staat effektiv regulieren. Die Regulierung muss zweierlei erreichen. Zum einen darf es kein Ausbeutungsmissbrauch geben. Die Netzmonopolisten dürfen nicht durch überhöhte Entgelte die Netznutzer und somit indirekt die Verbraucher belasten. Zum anderen darf es keinen Behinderungsmissbrauch geben. Die Monopolisten dürfen die Netzentgelte nicht missbräuchlich hoch setzen und mit Quersubventionierung die Konkurrenten beim Energiehandel verdrängen.

Wie die Regulierung der Netzmonopole konkret aussehen soll, lässt sich anhand dreier Fragen beantworten: Wann wird reguliert? Wie wird reguliert? Wer reguliert? Die wichtigste Frage ist, wann die Netzentgelte reguliert werden sollen. Vor oder nach einer Preiserhöhung? Die Antwort ist für Ordnungspolitiker klar. Vorher! Bevor das Kind in den Brunnen gefallen ist. Denn wir benötigen eine effektive Entgeltregulierung. Wir dürfen den Netzbetreibern keine missbräuchlichen Bewertungs- und Verhaltensspielräume in der Preisgestaltung lassen. Wir wollen Rechtssicherheit schaffen. Und wir wollen eine einfache Regulierung, die langwierige juristische Streitigkeiten vermeidet. Die Bundesregierung behauptet, eine Ex-ante-Regulierung sei organisatorisch nicht zu leisten. Das ist falsch, denn die nachträgliche Missbrauchsaufsicht bedingt erheblich mehr bürokratischen Aufwand.

Die zweite Frage lautet: Wie wird reguliert? Eine gesetzliche Vorfestlegung auf die Kalkulationsmethoden der Verbände wäre meines Erachtens falsch, weil sich die etablierten Energiemonopolisten so weiterhin eine goldene Nase verdienen können. Es darf keine gesetzliche Festschreibung der Kostenüberwälzung nach dem Prinzip der Nettosubstanzerhaltung geben. Erst in einer Verordnung sollte die Methode zur Entgeltfestsetzung geklärt werden. Außerdem muss die Methode zur Entgeltfestsetzung Anreizmechanismen zur Kostensenkung beinhalten. Die Entgelte müssen absolut transparent ermittelt werden. Und: Wir brauchen eine Stärkung des Vergleichsprinzips. Nicht der Durchschnitt der Netzentgelte, sondern die Entgelte der effizientesten Anbieter müssen Maßstab sein. Selbstverständlich müssen die Netzentgelte so bemessen werden, dass Netzbetreiber in der Lage und motiviert sind, die Leistungsfähigkeit der Netze dauerhaft zu sichern.

Wer regulieren soll, ist die dritte wichtige Frage. Die Ländermehrheit im Bundesrat fordert, die in den Ländern vorhandene Kompetenz zur Netzregulierung zu nutzen. Auch kann die Regulierungsbehörde des Bundes schlanker und effizienter arbeiten, wenn den Ländern die Regulierung der örtlichen und regionalen Verteilernetze übertragen wird.

Drei Fragen, drei klare Antworten. Wenn der Bundestag den Forderungen des Bundesrates folgt und die Netzmonopole in Zukunft wirksam kontrolliert werden, dann wird sich in Deutschland mehr Wettbewerb in der Strom- und Gaswirtschaft einstellen. Und sobald die Netzmonopole effektiv vorab reguliert werden, besteht die Option, die heute noch vorhandene Genehmigungspflicht der Haushaltstarife für Strom aufzugeben. Angesichts der breiten Zustimmung in der Öffentlichkeit sollte der Bundestag unseren Argumenten zustimmen und den Weg frei machen für niedrigere Energiepreise.

VI. Die Rolle des „Council of European Energy Regulators" bei der Durchsetzung von Verbraucherinteressen im liberalisierten Markt

Jorge Vasconcelos

Der Rat der Europäischen Energieregulierer (*Council of European Energy Regulators*, CEER) wurde im März 2000 gegründet und ist seit 2003 in Brüssel als Non-Profit-Organisation ansässig. Mit Aufnahme der neuen Mitgliedsstaaten in die EU erhöhte sich auch die Anzahl unserer Mitglieder auf 27. Der Rat der Europäischen Energieregulierer hat zwei Hauptziele. Zum einen fördert er die Zusammenarbeit unter den Regulierungsbehörden. Da alle Regulierungsbehörden sehr junge Institutionen sind, ist der Erfahrungs- und Informationsaustausch untereinander besonders wichtig. Zum anderen wollen wir die Zusammenarbeit mit der Europäischen Kommission, dem Parlament und anderen europäischen Institutionen intensivieren, um so schnell wie möglich einen Energiebinnenmarkt zu verwirklichen. Von einem solchen Energiebinnenmarkt sind wir noch weit entfernt.

Seit 1998 arbeiten wir bereits mit Vertretern der Verbraucher und der Industrie zusammen. Damals hat die Kommission mit den Regulierern das *European Electricity Regulatory* Forum, das so genannte Florenzforum und zwei Jahre später das „Madridforum" für Gas gegründet. Die Idee war, dass sich Kommission, Mitgliedsstaaten, Regulierer, Verbrauchervertreter und Industrie zusammensetzen, um über offene Fragen zu diskutieren. Diese Foren sind bis heute als Orte des Austausches erhalten geblieben. Nach der Einsetzung neuer Richtlinien für Strom und Gas sowie der Verordnung über den Stromhandel haben Rat und Kommission entschieden, dass diese Zusammenarbeit der Regulierer untereinander auch institutionell berücksichtigt werden soll und gründeten die *European Regulator's Group for Electricity and Gas* (ERGEG). Seit dem November 2003 gibt es also zwei Verbände auf europäischer Ebene, den CEER und die ERGEG, die gut miteinander zusammenarbeiten. Zwischen beiden Organisationen gibt es keine großen Unterschiede, und es wird sich in der Zukunft zeigen, ob wir beide behalten oder ob es nur noch eine Organisation geben wird. Für uns ist wichtig, dass bei dieser Zusammenarbeit niemand ausgeschlossen wird und die Verbraucher-Vertreter aktiv an diesen Prozessen teilnehmen. Dafür hat die ERGEG Richtlinien, die *„Public Guidelines on Consultation Practices"*, entwickelt und veröffentlicht.

Theorien über die Bedeutung einer unabhängigen Regulierung sind in Europa nicht neu. Schon in den dreißiger Jahren gab es Schriften über die Notwendigkeit einer unabhängigen Regulierung, beispielsweise von Walter Eucken. Während die

USA jedoch über mehr als 100 Jahre Praxiserfahrung mit unabhängiger Regulierung haben, hinkt Europa hinterher. Für die Bedeutung der Arbeit der Regulierer gibt es aus meiner Sicht mindestens fünf Gründe:

1. Die Monopolisten sind Informationsmonopolisten, und es ist sehr schwierig, an benötigte Informationen zu kommen. Doch ohne Information kann es keine wirksame Diskussion geben. Deshalb haben die Regulierer die Aufgabe, Informationen kontinuierlich und nachdrücklich zu sammeln und zu verbreiten sowie Transparenz zu schaffen.

2. Die Regulierer sollen Gerechtigkeit und Effizienz herstellen und sichern. Wenn die Netzentgeltgebühren richtig kalkuliert wurden, dann müssen wir diese Tarife an alle Netznutzer weitergeben. Die Netzkunden, einschließlich der Endkunden, sollen genau das zahlen, was sie zahlen müssen. Man nennt das *cost reflective tariffs*. Leider gibt es in vielen Ländern noch Quersubventionierungen, auch in Deutschland. Eine Quersubventionierung ist nicht nur die Subventionierung zwischen verschiedenen Aktivitäten, wie zum Beispiel von Erzeugung, Übertragung und Verteilung – wenn man die Erzeugungskosten auf die Netzkosten umschlägt, gibt es selbstverständlich Wettbewerbsverzerrung. Aber es gibt noch eine andere Art der Quersubventionierung, die sehr raffiniert und schädlich sowohl für den Wettbewerb als auch für Effizienz und Gerechtigkeit ist: die Quersubventionierung zwischen verschiedenen Kundenkategorien. Um diese Quersubventionierungen zu identifizieren, braucht man Daten, Informationen, mathematische Modelle und eine Ex-ante-Regulierung. Eine Preisfestsetzung reicht nicht aus, um sicher zu gehen, dass es keine Wettbewerbsverzerrungen gibt. Und Wettbewerbsverzerrungen verhindern Effizienz und Gerechtigkeit.

3. Die Regulierer sollen den Wettbewerb fördern und als Marktaufsicht fungieren, weil die Energiemärkte sehr komplex sind. Marktregeln müssen sowohl für *wholesale markets* als auch für *retail markets* robust und solide sein.

4. Die Regulierer sollen die Möglichkeit haben, Beschwerden zu bearbeiten und bei Konflikten als Vermittler aufzutreten.

5. Die Regulierer sollen die aktive Teilnahme der Verbraucher am Regulierungsprozess sicher stellen. In Portugal haben wir zum Beispiel zwei Gremien in der Regulierungsbehörde: ein Beratungsgremium und ein Tarifgremium. Im Tarifausschuss sind die Verbraucher und die regulierten Unternehmen vertreten, im Beratungsausschuss sind noch andere vertreten, zum Beispiel das Umweltministerium und die Kommunen. Wenn es beispielsweise um Tarife geht, müssen wir einen Vorschlag in den Tarifausschuss einreichen. Die Mitglieder haben

dann 30 Kalendertage Zeit, um sich zu äußern. Die endgültige Entscheidung müssen wir dann in einem Gutachten veröffentlichen und darin begründen, warum wir die Vorschläge angenommen haben oder nicht. *Reasons giving* ist selbstverständlich sehr wichtig, um eine transparente Regulierung zu haben.

Das sind die wesentlichen Gründe, warum eine unabhängige Regulierung aus meiner Sicht für die Energieverbraucher wichtig ist. Die weiteren Aufgaben der Regulierer kann man in ihren Statuten nachlesen.

Zum Schluss einige Bemerkungen zum Energiebinnenmarkt. Auf europäischer Ebene erlangt die Regulierung der Energiemärkte eine immer größere Bedeutung. Wir haben seit dem 1. Juli 2004 einen konsistenten Gesetzesrahmen, der weiterzuentwickeln ist. Aus meiner Sicht gibt es zwei Gruppen von offenen Fragen. Zum einen gibt es nicht genug Leitungen und Übertragungskapazität, um einen Binnenmarkt verwirklichen zu können. Wenn wir aber einen Strombinnenmarkt und einen Gasbinnenmarkt haben wollen, dann müssen wir den Bau von neuen Leitungen beschleunigen. Es gibt nationale beziehungsweise regionale Märkte und dort bestehen die Probleme mit den Netzzugängen nach wie vor. In Deutschland hat der Regulierer mit seiner Arbeit noch nicht angefangen. In der Schweiz gibt es überhaupt noch keinen Regulierer. Und die Schweiz spielt eine zentrale Rolle in Europa. Außerdem ist die Zusammenarbeit unter den Netzbetreibern noch nicht optimal, weil sie sich noch nicht an die neuen Gegebenheiten angepasst hat. Hier brauchen wir neue Regeln für die Zusammenarbeit unter den Netzbetreibern. Unter den Netzbetreibern sollte es keinen Wettbewerb, sondern eine gute Zusammenarbeit geben, denn bei schlechter Zusammenarbeit kommt es zu solchen Blackouts wie vor einem Jahr in Italien oder neulich in Luxemburg. Diese neue Art der Zusammenarbeit der Netzbetreiber können wir gestalten. Wir wissen, wie wir diese einzelnen Fragen behandeln und wie wir das alles verbessern können. Seit dem 1. Juli verfügen wir über die Instrumente dazu.

Die andere Gruppe der offenen Fragen hat mit der Industriestruktur zu tun. So ist die Anwendung des Wettbewerbsrechts und der Wettbewerbsinstrumente in Europa nicht einheitlich und nicht immer konsistent. Beides behindert die Marktentwicklung. Um diese Konsistenz zu erhöhen, muss sich die Zusammenarbeit zwischen den Energieregulierern, der Wettbewerbsbehörde und der Kommission weiterentwickeln.

In meiner Funktion als Regulierer muss ich oft drei Fragen – nach der Versorgungssicherheit, den Preisen und der Integration der Märkte – beantworten. Die erste Frage lautet, ob die Liberalisierung bedeutet, dass unsere Versorgungssicherheit in Europa in Gefahr ist. Die Antwort ist: „Nein". Man sollte dabei klar zwischen politischen Maßnahmen, die Einfluss auf die Versorgungssicherheit haben und dem technischen Aspekt der Versorgungssicherheit unterscheiden. Um die zweite Frage nach den Preissteigerungen beantworten zu können beziehungsweise um über Preise konstruktiv diskutieren zu können, braucht man gute Informationen. Zum einen gibt es Steuern und weitere Preisfaktoren, die nichts mit der Energieerzeugung, -verteilung und -übertragung zu tun haben. Außerdem sind nach der Regulierung die Netzkosten für Strom tatsächlich in vielen Ländern stark gesunken. Schließlich ist die Behauptung, dass wenn Kohle-, Erdgas- und Ölpreise steigen, auch die Energiepreise steigen müssen, zum Teil zwar richtig. Zugleich werden die Energiepreise aber auch von Marktstrukturen beeinflusst, und hier sehen wir in Europa durchaus Verbesserungsbedarf. Auf die dritte Frage, ob wir bei einem Energiebinnenmarkt auch nur einen einzigen Stromnetzbetreiber, einen einzigen Gasnetzbetreiber und einen einzigen Regulierer in Europa brauchen, antworte ich mit „Nein". Im Moment brauchen wir keinen europäischen Regulierer. „Non sunt multiplicanda entia praeter necessitatem" – wir müssen die Zahl der Institutionen nicht unnötig erhöhen – um den großen englischen Philosophen William von Ockham frei zu zitieren. Doch das soll nicht als Ausrede dienen, im Rahmen der Regulierung und der Anwendung des Wettbewerbsrechts nichts zu unternehmen. Es gibt noch viel Handlungsspielraum zwischen nationaler Behörde und Europäischer Kommission.

VII. Representing consumers' interests in the liberalised gas and electricity markets – the British model

Edward Blades

The Department of Trade and Industry's Economic Regulation Team

The Economic Regulation Team of the Department and Trade and Industry (DTI) provides a focus within the DTI and Government for addressing cross-cutting issues in the different regulated sectors, and the development of economic regulation policy. This is important because the liberalisation of different sectors was undertaken at different times by different departments of Government. There is therefore a need to achieve some sort of cohesive view and to bring a cross-cutting capability to bear on regulatory issues.

The DTI report "Consumer Representation in Regulated Industries"[1] is one of the outputs of the Economic Regulation Team. I do not pretend to be an expert in consumer representation. But I have been involved in the UK privatisation programme and in the regulation of utilities for around 15 years, so I can understand the perspective of the role of consumer representation in the proper regulation of liberalised markets.

The British experience with the liberalisation of utility industries

When I saw the brochure for this conference, I was surprised by the very bold statement that "...of all European countries, Britain has done the most to press ahead with the liberalisation of services of general interest. But the British experience has shown that liberalised markets do not automatically produce efficient customer-orientated services".

This encapsulates the issues very well. The UK has certainly done much to press ahead. It has not been an easy process to undertake, although it has brought great benefits and I am happy to share our experience with you. But in doing so, I propose to share our learning experience, as this is a process which we continue to monitor and review. This is in fact just a way of saying that we do not necessarily

---

[1] Siehe Zweiter Abschnitt

have it absolutely right yet, but we are trying very hard. We also try to learn from the experiences of other countries and are ready to adopt good ideas wherever we can find them.

I will now briefly explain the different stages of utility market liberalisation in the UK. The process of liberalisation started some 20 years ago with the telecoms and gas markets. Water and electricity followed over the next seven years. Some degree of competition was established in telecoms from the outset in 1984. The initial duopoly approach was perhaps rather disappointing in the extent of the competition introduced. A critical revision of arrangements and the emergence for example of cable operators and mobile telephony has now brought more extensive competition to the market. Arrangements initially established in water, what we call "inset appointments", were also less effective in establishing competition than was wished. New provisions and recent legislation, particularly the Water Act of 2003, should provide greater opportunity for competition. In terms of supply, electricity and gas have been fully competitive since 1999, but this does not mean that the advent of the competitive market has been without problems. In postal services, one of the regulators has just announced that the market will be fully open to competition as of 1 January 2006, some 15 months earlier then previously planned. Royal Mail remains a state-owned monopoly at present, and that presents special difficulties in the market.

Liberalisation and consumers

Two of the key outcomes that we looked for from the liberalisation programme were significantly increased efficiency and better prices and services for consumers. How could this be achieved? The approach that we have generally taken has been to introduce competition wherever possible and to rely on independent regulation where there are natural monopolies or where competitive markets will only emerge over time. But until fully mature competitive markets are established, we need to provide a strong voice for the consumer – a robust champion of consumers' interests. It is worth considering the general framework adopted for market liberalisation. The best approach, which we adopted latterly, but which we certainly did not follow in the early market liberalisations, was to restructure state-owned businesses to provide a firm basis for competition to become established. We established an independent economic regulator in each sector, ensuring that the operation of the businesses was removed from political interference. This was important in order to permit commercial freedom and to attract investment. As part of the overall regulatory framework for each sector, a consumer body was established to represent the interests of consumers to companies, to the regulator and to the government. The bodies are charged with acting as the voice of consumers, and with helping consumers to resolve problems. These bodies were established by statute in the same piece of legislation that also privatised the industry and set up the regulatory body.

Market liberalisation has led to significant improvements in efficiency and competitiveness. In some sectors liberalisation has been a catalyst for new entrants to bring greater choice to customers, offering new products and driving the adoption of new technology. The combination of competition and regulation has delivered lower prices to consumers than would otherwise have been the case. In some markets, it has meant significant reductions in prices. In others, it has minimised the price increases necessary to fund essential new investment in these essential services. But where competition has only recently been established, as in gas and electricity, it has brought certain difficulties for consumers. There were cases of failure by some companies to adopt high standards of conduct when selling services in the competitive market. Those companies who adopted high pressure sales techniques were rightly censured. In other sectors, where competition is yet to be established, consumers face a virtual monopoly provider of the essential service, and much greater emphasis must be placed on the role of the regulator and the role of the consumer body.

I have mentioned both the regulator and the consumer body. But I am often asked why we need both. Sectoral regulators have very important customer-facing statutory duties, and this sometimes takes a form of an explicit primary objective to protect the interest of consumers. But otherwise it can take the form of an objective linked to the provision or the preservation of an essential service, which is of course in the interest of consumers. These are important duties. But the regulators also have wider duties such as ensuring that a regulated business can finance its regulated activities. So there must be some element of balancing these various duties. Consequently, the role of the consumer body as a consumer advocate provides the essential consumer focus within the regulatory framework. It is important to maintain that essential consumer focus because of the particular challenges consumers face in a liberalised market.

I will now take a look at some of these challenges. Although liberalisation can provide choices, it can also foster uncertainty for consumers. That uncertainty may be rooted, to some extent, in misunderstanding over how the market works or how choice can be exercised. There is also an element of inertia which can reinforce that problem. Consumers may not be quick to exercise choice in a market. Uncertainty can be caused by information problems or by company behaviour. Customers need good, impartial advice about how to compare prices, how to exercise choice and how to deal with difficulties which they encounter – for example when changing suppliers or with miss-selling. Different groups of customers – particularly vulnerable groups of customers – can find that a competitive market provides benefits but that the biggest benefits may be enjoyed by other groups of consumers. Security of supply is also a real priority, although if you asked consumers what they are most interested in, they would be interested in having low prices and assume that security of supply has automatically been dealt with. In all of these issues the role of the consumer body is essential in providing the consumer with the best possible experience of making choices in a liberalised market.

The role of consumer bodies in regulated markets

Having established the need for an independent consumer voice within the regulatory framework, some of the specific functions which need to be performed by a consumer body include the following. Consumer bodies need to take a strategic view of consumer interests. They need to be able to look beyond the immediate difficulties in the market and work with companies, the regulator and government to prepare for medium and long-term developments in the market. They have an important role in helping consumers resolve complaints and to provide information to consumers to enable them to make good decisions in the market. I mentioned that market liberalisation may impact on vulnerable groups of consumers. It may be that they can take advantage of the very best savings on offer in a competitive market or that they are in danger of losing out through competitive markets leading to cost-reflective pricing. That again is an area in which the role of a consumer body is important.

The findings of the DTI report "Consumer Representation in Regulated Industries"[2]

The DTI undertook a consumer representation project in 2004 to find out how consumer bodies were doing and whether we could establish best practice. I am happy – but not particularly surprised – to say that we found firm evidence of sustained commitment by all of the consumer bodies by helping or forcing through the delivery of measures to correct problems in the market. There are many individual examples of the positive influence without which many customers would

---

2 Siehe Zweiter Abschnitt.

have been disadvantaged. We found, however, that Energywatch and Postwatch were labouring under an extremely unfair burden of complaints from customers. They deserve considerable credit for helping so many customers resolve complaints about service. But it does mean that Energywatch was devoting 41 per cent of its budget to handling complaints, and Postwatch 18 per cent. We considered that this was an unfair burden, that the companies themselves should be handling complaints effectively and that resources could be used by the consumer bodies in other more productive ways.

Each of the consumer bodies we dealt with provided many examples of best practice. We encourage them to work together more closely and to share best practice and identify ways in which joint efforts could bring rewards to consumers. There was clear enthusiasm for joint working and I think Energywatch and Postwatch could establish a new umbrella organisation, a consumer action network, to provide for this sort of cooperation.

We suggested that consumer bodies should also seek to establish working relationships with regulators and companies. It is not unusual or necessarily undesirable for consumer bodies, regulators and even government to have significantly different views on any given issue. But much can be achieved through working closer together, with each other and with industry. That is not a remark directed just at the consumer bodies, it certainly applies to government departments as well.

The project team did wonder whether, in the longer term, the use of ombudsmen schemes could help provide the necessary incentive for companies to deal with their own complaints effectively. We also wondered whether the separate consumer bodies established for each liberalised utility market and for postal services, each with their own regional organisations, provided consumers with an unnecessarily fragmented approach to dealing with essential services. We are currently undertaking a public consultation on our consumer strategy which includes seeking views on whether it would be a good idea to think about the wider application of ombudsman schemes, and whether it would be advantageous in the longer term to consolidate sectoral consumer bodies.

Key features of the UK model

Some of the key features of the UK model include the establishment of a separate independent regulator and a separate consumer body for each of the liberalised sectors. There have been developments in sectoral consumer representation over time and indeed Energywatch was formed less than four years ago to consolidate the previously separate consumer bodies for gas and electricity. That consolidation extended to the separate regulators for electricity and gas also coming together to form a single regulatory body. WaterVoice will also undergo reform in 2005. The changes provided in the Water Act put WaterVoice on an independent basis. We try to learn from experience and we try to update the regulatory framework and institutions as necessary. I think it is important – as with all aspects of the regulatory framework – that we do not get carried away and try to do this too often because changes can bring uncertainty and cause confusion.

Lessons to be learnt from the British experience

I will now finish with a suggestion about decisions facing colleagues in Germany. My understanding is that the existing regulator for post and telecommunications in Germany will gain responsibility for ensuring fair access to gas and electricity networks. I did wonder whether it would be possible to establish a common consumer body for all these sectors and whether that could provide a useful focus for consumers. This is because for essential services such as utility services or postal services, each one of us is a consumer of all of these services.

VIII. The watchdogs: WaterVoice

Sheila Reiter

WaterVoice's aim

WaterVoice's aim is "To be the most effective and powerful voice of water and sewerage customers in England and Wales by promoting and advocating their interests in respect of price and service with the water industry, the economic and quality regulators, the Government, and in the European Union".

Our aim is simple to define but not always easy to achieve. You will note that we refer to customers. The household and business customers we represent are not simply water **consumers**; they pay for a service and expect to receive a good quality service and value for money. We look to water companies to work hard to keep their customers happy, even though most customers have no choice of which water company provides their water and sewerage services.

Water industry: structure and regulation

The water industry in England and Wales was privatised in 1989 under the Thatcher Government. Originally there were 39 companies, since reduced through mergers and acquisitions to 24 companies (some of which have foreign owners including French, Chinese, Malaysian and German, with RWE the owner of our largest water company, Thames Water).

Water companies operate in practice as regional monopolies in the areas they serve. Competition is almost non-existent with only a very few large business customers having switched from one company to another.

When the industry was privatised a regulatory regime was set up comprising:

1. An economic regulator Ofwat, which controls the prices companies can charge and protects customers' interests
2. An environmental regulator, The Environment Agency
3. A drinking water regulator, The Drinking Water Inspectorate
4. A customer representative organisation, WaterVoice

The average household bill 2004/05 is 361 Euro, comprising 170 Euro for water and 191 Euro for sewerage. Water bills have risen in real terms by nearly 25 per cent since 1989. But between 1989 and 2005 70 billion Euro, all funded by customers, has been invested by the water industry in drinking water quality and in improvements to the water environment to meet European Union standards.

Service to customers has also steadily improved to the point where for example:

1. Only 0.06 per cent of properties were at risk of low water pressure
2. Only 0.05 per cent of customers experienced unplanned interruptions to supply lasting over 12 hours
3. 99.8 per cent of written complaints were answered by water companies in 10 days

WaterVoice's structure and work

WaterVoice is a national water consumer organisation with a regional structure. We have ten regional committees, nine in England and one for Wales. The ten Committee Chairmen form the WaterVoice National Council. The Council has six policy sub-groups dealing with charging, complaints management, competition and industry structure, European issues, customer research and standards of service. The WaterVoice Council and the committees are supported by 65 staff in our head office and eight regional offices.

The Committee Chairmen are appointed by the Director General of Ofwat who also appoints the Committee Members on the recommendation of the relevant Chairman. The Chairman and Members are eligible for re-appointment but do not serve for more than ten years. The aim is to manage turnover on the committees so that there is a mix of experienced members and new people. Chairman and members are expected to live or work in their Committee's region. They are appointed in a personal capacity and not to represent a pressure group or other organisation. All Committees have people from a range of backgrounds from across each region with a reasonable balance of men and women and people from ethnic minority groups.

WaterVoice has statutory duties to represent the interest of all water and sewerage customers, household, business and others. We investigate complaints from customers about their water companies and in the vast majority of cases achieve a fair and reasonable outcome. As a measure of our success since we were set up we have obtained 13 million Euro in compensation and rebates to resolve complaints.

We work closely with the economic regulator Ofwat. We are consulted by Ofwat on all policy proposals and we provide each other with information about the water companies. The Director General of Ofwat attends every meeting of the WaterVoice National Council to report on his work and to answer questions.

We work with the water companies individually and at national level, and with other organisations at regional, national and European level. In representing customers we operate at national or regional level depending on the issue. We hold regular meetings in public in the regions and publish minutes of our meetings. We produce a work programme and we report on what we have achieved in our Annual Report.

We aim to:

- Understand customers' views – we listen to customers and identify their expectations and priorities about price, service and value for money.
- Give customers a voice – we promote and advocate the interest of all customers, balancing the interests of different groups where necessary, taking account of the needs of vulnerable customers and others with special needs.
- Influence decisions and policies – we seek to ensure that the water industry, the regulators, the Government and the European Union properly consider customers' interests.
- Promote awareness and accessibility – we want customers to know we exist to represent their interests, and make it easy for them to contact us.

We are never short of work; instead we have to choose our priorities, focussing on those issues that most affect customers and where we can have the most influence. Currently our big issues include the 2004 price review, European Union policies, plans for a new Consumer Council for Water, water charging and metering (currently only 24 per cent of households in England and Wales are metered), developing a competitive market for business customers, debt and affordability, and eliminating the misery for customers of sewer flooding.

2004 price review

Ofwat reviews and sets limits every five years on how much the water companies in England and Wales can charge their customers each year. We are currently involved in the 2004 Review, which sets price limits for the period 2005 to 2010. The water companies asked Ofwat for increases of nearly 30 per cent on average over the five year period plus inflation (on the current average bill of 361 Euro).

We aim to ensure that Ofwat in particular understands and responds to the views of customers. We seek a realistic approach to price increases that achieves a fair balance between further improvements to the environment and those areas that customers themselves have identified as priorities. Customers want a safe, reliable and continuous water supply and better maintenance of the sewerage network, especially to prevent sewer flooding of homes and gardens.

Ofwat in its draft decisions announced in August cut the companies' proposals by over half to an average increase of 13 per cent over five years. This is still a significant increase and will cause problems for customers on low incomes.

WaterVoice and Europe

EU water policy affects all EU citizens, and especially the size of their water bill. The WaterVoice European Group, which I chair, focuses on EU water and consumer policy issues. We ensure the customers' voice is heard by the UK Government, the European Commission (DG Environment and DG Sanco) and the European Parliament (in particular the Environment Committee). On behalf of customers we press for better cost benefit analysis before decisions are taken in Brussels. We want the interests of customers, who ultimately pay higher water bills for improvements to be taken into account alongside the interests of environmental and other groups.

Current issues include:

1. Revision of the 1976 Bathing Water Directive – we welcome the balanced and sensible approach taken to new standards and the strengthening of the provisions on making information available to the public about bathing water quality.
2. Competition in the water sector – we await the outcome of the Commission's report of its review, which is due at the end of the year.
3. Services of General Interest – in response to last year's Green Paper we pressed the Commission to focus on consumers in developing any proposals for new EU regulation of water sector and other utilities.

A new Consumer Council for Water

Under the Water Act 2003 WaterVoice will be replaced by a new independent Consumer Council for Water, similar to Energywatch and Postwatch. Among other improvements we will have a new and better resourced Head Office to strengthen our customer research capacity and our advocacy role. We will also have for the first time statutory powers to obtain and publish information from water companies and from Ofwat. These changes are due to take effect on 1 October 2005.

Conclusion

In this presentation I have been able to provide only a taste of what WaterVoice's work as a consumer watchdog brings to the regulation of the water industry and the protection of customers' interests in England and Wales. There is much more information to be found on our website www.ofwat.gov.uk.

IX.   The watchdogs: Postwatch

Gregor McGregor

The British postal market

The postal market has a very different set of market circumstances to the water, gas and electricity industries. In the UK postal market there are two directives which govern the market. Interestingly enough, the UK postal market is currently liberalised but not yet privatised. Within this overall framework there are four constituent parts: The Royal Mail Group (which is no longer a nationalised industry but a public limited company, though the shares are not quoted on the stock exchange), the economic regulator Postcomm, the separate consumer body Postwatch, and the shareholder, which is the Department of Trade and Industry.

The ideas behind Postwatch

The UK has a long experience of utility regulation, going back some 20 years and covering significant parts of the UK economy. The system of regulation has long been dominated by the economic regulator. However the economic regulator is often remote and not especially customer friendly. Underpinned by a strong commitment from the current government to improve customer representation, this state of affairs created the need for a separate representative for customers in addition to the economic regulator. Furthermore, I am convinced that a consumer representative adds value to the system and does not simply subtract costs from it.

Postwatch's structure, financing and functions

Postwatch is regionally based and has nine offices throughout the UK. The regional basis of our structure is very important and was deliberately put in place in order to counter the remoteness of the economic regulator. We consciously set out to communicate with as many postal customers as we can. And to that end, not only do we have these nine offices, but each of those offices has its own representative group, often with ten or twelve members. And they in turn have focus groups, regular meetings and a whole range of contacts within local communities and groups interested in postal matters. We have 14 members on our council. Nine of those are the regional chairmen, four are national members and one is our chairman. These members are appointed by the Minister for Trade and Industry.

We have a staff of 120 and a budget of about 20 million Euro. That is paid for by licence fees from postal operators. One of the reasons we have 120 members of staff is our complaints function. When we started three years ago, we were dealing with about 10,000 complaints a year. One of the things which has really surprised us is the way in which the number of complaints has completely taken off. Complaints increased from 10,000 to 240,000 in three years. And frankly, we have been struggling to keep up with this demand and it goes to show just how much frustration there is with the postal service in the UK. Before we were set up, there was no independent voice that could speak on behalf of customers, and customers did not have an independent body they could complain to.

Another major function of Postwatch is the research function. We take this very seriously because for a consumer council to be effective, it has to be thoroughly researched in everything it says and does. In this area we look at issues such as pricing, how competition is being introduced and whether or not it is benefiting the market place. Another issue is whether a particular service benefits certain customers at the expense of others. We also assist the regulator in looking into issues such as licensing policy. A key part of our research is trying to understand precisely what customers want and need from their postal service. This should be seen against a background of circumstances were the Royal Mail has been the ultimate government monopoly for some 350 years, and people do not tend to think in terms of what postal services they want. Instead they tend to think in terms of what postal services they have always had and whether they will continue to get them.

A unique feature of postal regulation is the post office branch network. It is an accident of history that we have inherited some 17,000 or 18,000 post office branches. This causes a problem because these branches are dearly loved by customers, or voters for that matter. The trouble is that those customers and voters do not really visit or spend any money in these branches. They therefore lose a significant amount of money every year.

Our mission is to promote, protect and develop the interests of customers. We aim to represent all customers. Interestingly enough in the postal market, this does not just mean those who pay for the stamp and send a letter, but also those who receive (or frequently don't receive) mail sent to them. So our role is to deal with complaints, inform customers – or indeed the latest buzzword is "empower" customers – and undertake research. We also have a particular role towards disadvantaged customers, which is one of the factors shared across all the UK's consumer's councils.

Postwatch's role within the regulatory system

There are of course tensions within the structures that have been created. We sometimes have to work at odds with the existing players, and the trick is to try and do this constructively. We have, for example, tension with the government as the shareholder. Obviously, the shareholder interest is to maximise profits (or in Royal Mail's case, to minimise losses). And it is also the body that sponsors not only ourselves but the economic regulator as well. When the two of us are working well together, our joint objective is to make the best possible deal for customers. But there is also tension with the regulator. You may well be familiar with the concept of "regulatory capture". In the postal market it is interesting, because to the extent where there are independent regulators, the idea of "capture" seems to indicate that they put up a fight. But many of the economic or independent regulators in the European postal market are so close to industry that "capture" is not quite the right word. It is thus important that there should be a consumer body which asks the regulator whether the interests of the management or of shareholders have come to predominate their thinking.

Interestingly enough, we have been generally welcomed by politicians. One of the reasons for this is that we are often the soft face of what are very hard decisions. The postal world, because it has been a monopoly for so long, needs to be thoroughly modernised. Customers do not like this because it means changes – and possible reductions – to existing services. Major cost savings and price efficiency are however essential if the Royal Mail and other post operators across Europe are to survive. We therefore take our role seriously in trying to engage with customers, explaining that there are very good reasons for the changes, and that customers will ultimately reap the benefits in terms of better service. Exactly the same argument applies to post office closures because the post office network has to shrink if it is going to have any future at all.

Obviously, the monopolists do not like us terribly much, but over the three or four years that we have been running, we have gained a grudging respect, although it sometimes seems to be more about grudge than respect. But that is what you expect in a constructive but tense relationship with a monopolist.

Current challenges

We are currently involved in a major quality of service issue. As the consumer body, we have set certain quality of service targets for Royal Mail for the past three years. They were initially achieving nine out of 16 of these targets. This then went down to three out of 16 of the targets. And now Royal Mail has decided it is not going to meet any of the targets. Interestingly, there is an inverse relationship between the failure to deliver a decent level of service and what has happened to the loss-making, now profitability, of the Royal Mail Group. It was initially losing 1,800 million Euro then they managed to halve that loss, and last year they managed to make a small profit. One of the major issues we have with the management of Royal Mail at the moment is that that they have returned to profitability, but only by denying customers the quality of service they expect and pay for. That in turn drives up the number of complaints. And one of the reasons why complaints have increased from 10,000 to 240,000 a year is because the quality of service delivered by Royal Mail is as poor as it is.

This brings us to the question of compensation and financial penalties. We have been quite successful in putting in place a compensation regime which covers both private and business users of the postal system. For this past year, Royal Mail should pay compensation of about 140 million Euro as a result of its failure to guarantee quality of service standards. But I suspect there may well be a major legal dispute before they actually pay out the money.

The bigger picture

If we look at things on a larger scale, the opening up of the market is gaining speed, certainly in the UK if not across Europe, where people are still discussing whether it is the right thing to do. It is however one thing to remove the legal inhibitions to competition, but it is quite another thing to actually see effective competition on the ground. Much of the discussion about the gas and electricity markets shows the problems that can emerge for consumers even where there are markets which are theoretically competitive. What we have seen in the UK is higher prices and a reduced quality of service. Royal Mail is having to turn itself around and there have been some 30,000 job losses over the past year, with probably more to come. There have also been major changes to the way in which the Royal Mail operates, matters like delivery times, the frequency of deliveries, changes to its antiquated product range and post office closures, of which there have been 3,000 over the past two years, each one of which involves extensive local consultation. It is therefore critical to have a regional network which understands the locality in which it works. Another recurring issue is privatisation and whether it will happen. We really do not know the answer at the moment, but I suspect the government does not want to become involved in a privatisation debate this side of the 2005 general election.

We as a consumer council believe competition is the best way forward, because competition gives customers a choice. If there is choice, this drives efficiency, helps innovation and provides customers with the ability to choose value-for-money services that they want. The UK was originally planning full liberalisation by April 2007. I am glad to say the regulator has recently announced it is going to advance that timetable, not least because of the poor service the Royal Mail is delivering to its customers.

X. The watchdogs: Energywatch

Allan Asher

Liberalisation of British energy markets

When the energy markets were liberalised in the UK in the 1990s it became clear that consumers were not going to be the beneficiaries. The profits of energy companies escalated, disconnections hit 30,000 a year and the service to customers declined. The Government's aim of injecting innovation and efficiency into the industry was, instead, characterised by innovative mis-selling and very efficient profiteering. The liberalisation strategy lacked two essential elements: adequate regulatory control and consumer protection. In fact the impact on consumers had not been considered. What was now going wrong for most domestic energy users was catastrophic for vulnerable consumers such as pensioners and the chronically sick. They were piling up energy debts, and forced to have pre-payment meters which extracted payment towards that debt before they were given access to power. Thousands of families were left without heat, light or power by companies able to enter their homes to disconnect supply. Business users found themselves locked into contracts and soaring costs for electricity and gas. Liberalisation was producing a few fat industry winners and a large number of losers, including new market entrants who were unable to compete against incumbent producers and suppliers. In fact, competition was stifled. Energy was certainly not 'free'.

The Government failed to promote competition, failed to protect consumers and failed to appreciate that energy is not just another commodity. Gas and electricity are essential to modern life. Surprisingly, the Government had not understood either that consumers are a fundamental component of competitive markets. Consumers making good choices apply the necessary pressure for innovation, efficiency and the drive for a competitive edge: All the things liberalisation was intended to achieve towards building a healthy national economy.

Many studies have shown that competitive markets do increase productivity and bring economic gain. But why stop there? Competitive markets can also bring benefits for consumers **if** they are properly regulated and transparent. Reduced prices are the most obvious gain, but there are many others such as improved customer service and new products, **if** the market is genuinely competitive and consumers are able to have some control in it. They are not well served, however, by abundant offers of opaque deals. Consumers cannot make sensible choices in any market without adequate – and accurate – information about what they will get for their money. One of the most successful ways energywatch helps consumers is to give them access to up-to-date information on energy companies and a comparison of their prices. Half of energy users in the UK have exercised their choice and switched supplier at least once in the past few years – an exceptionally high rate by international standards – and they are making significant savings. One of our priorities is to encourage more people to switch to companies that offer not just price savings but better information, more accurate billing and improved services.

Establishing a regulator and watchdog

The turn-around from the chaos of the early years of liberalisation started with a new Government strategy to motivate – and control – the markets using regulation, law enforcement and the pressure of consumer choice. A market regulator, Ofgem, was established and given the power to fine companies or remove their operating licences for breaches of the law, including consumer protection law. energywatch was the first consumer watchdog of its kind to be established by statute. Both bodies protect and promote the interests of consumers but we work from different perspectives. energywatch talks directly to consumers, educates them and helps to resolve their complaints. We look for systemic solutions to some of their problems such as fuel poverty. The numbers with poor access to energy have fallen by half from five million, but even a slight rise in prices will begin to reverse this trend. energywatch represents consumers at Government policy discussions on issues such as this. Ofgem, meanwhile, regulates the markets and the industry. We share the objective of making the markets work well for consumers and we do this by ensuring that anti-competitive practices are removed, and behaviour detrimental to consumers is dealt with.

energywatch is able, from the vast amount of information it collects from consumers, to alert the regulator to problems. We are able to advise Government and policy makers about the likely impact on consumers of new regulation and law. We are particularly successful in gaining the support of Members of Parliament for our campaigns and for changes in the law. We use the media to advance the rights of energy consumers. But we are also pragmatic and recognise that more regulation leads to more cost for industry, and ultimately higher prices for consumers. We want our energy suppliers to be successful and to enjoy profits that allow investment. That is why we are increasingly talking directly to companies to try to resolve problems without legal or regulatory action, and why we are developing standards and codes of practice to encourage and help the industry to regulate itself. We have a system for praising good performance and we have a system for "naming and shaming" poor performance. Our aim is to educate the companies to understand that good customer service brings rewards and savings. An industry summit, hosted by energywatch and Ofgem, convinced companies of the need for change when we revealed that 53,000 erroneous customer transfers a week need to be expensively and manually corrected by company staff. Savings in not having to make compensation payments, savings in not having to pay high financial penalties for mis-selling and savings from retaining customers because they are happy with the service they are getting.

Results

A competitive retail market in GB has reduced energy prices by up to 50 per cent since liberalisation. Prices are beginning to rise again, largely we believe, because of less than competitive wholesale prices. We have been heavily involved in the Ofgem review of the marketing licence condition and investigations into the competitiveness of the energy markets. In January 2004, we commissioned follow up research to that undertaken in 2002 on "Charges, Costs and Market Power in the Deregulated UK Electricity Retail Market". The researchers found evidence of incumbent market power being exercised in the domestic electricity market. The research also concluded that substantial market power remains and that Ofgem needs to remain alert to potential abuse, on grounds of both efficiency and equity. We have asked Ofgem to undertake a comprehensive review of the market and look at the impact on consumers of consolidation and vertical integration. We are also campaigning for a Europe-wide investigation of competition in the energy markets.

Consumers are switching supplier but research commissioned by energywatch indicates that householders could save millions of euros if they were more confident about changing supplier. We have campaigned successfully to remove some of the obstructions companies use to prevent or delay switching. Parliamentary support has enabled families in debt to one company to change to another, cheaper, provider.

Disconnections are down significantly from the 70,000 over three years to the end of 2003. Just 1,650 were recorded for the first half of this year. We are continuing to campaign for an end to disconnections for vulnerable consumers and improvements to the processes the industry goes through before deciding to disconnect. Preventing debt is part of this. Our view is that an affluent society has no excuse for leaving families without heat, light or power and no excuse for the tragedies that have resulted from this. We have put the issue onto the political agenda and the industry is finally beginning to accept that it has a social responsibility towards its customers. Companies have a duty to promote the Priority Services Register which provides special help to those who are registered as vulnerable. energywatch played a significant role in the creation of two company trust funds, set up by British Gas and EDF, to pay the bills of those unable to pay them. The fund also provides them with debt counselling and advice on using energy efficiently.

Complaints issues

energywatch receives a million requests a year for information or help. An increasing number of these are from business energy users. In 2002/3 around 13,000 of the 100,000 complaints we receive every year were about mis-selling by electricity and gas companies or their agents. Consumers were put under pressure, often on their own doorsteps, to switch supplier. Promises of cheaper fuel were found to be false. Some householders discovered that their supplier had changed without their knowledge or agreement. A high profile media campaign, a new marketing code of practice and evidence to Ofgem of mis-selling, which resulted in financial penalties for some of the worst practitioners, reduced the number of complaints to 400. We are now collecting details of compensation paid to consumers to ensure that suitable amounts are available for all breaches of the marketing code.

Billing is another major problem area. In 2002/3 we received 43,000 complaints about inaccurate bills. Many of them had been estimated by the energy company. Invariably they were overestimates. An energywatch-commissioned survey revealed that estimated billing had put at least two million households in debt to energy companies. One in four could not pay the debt and were at risk of disconnection. A campaign for better billing has reduced to problem – earlier this year complaints were down to 10,000 – but we are determined to resolve the problem entirely. energywatch is driving the development of a national standard for energy billing. We are working with the British Standards Institute (BSI) and, internationally, work is going on at the ISO to produce an energy standard based on our national draft. We are asking Ofgem to consider a billing Licence Condition on companies.

A Rights for Energy Users charter gives us a strategic framework for identifying and prioritising our activities and we work with many organisations to deliver education and help to vulnerable groups through our Reachout programme.

The future

The future will be a European and a global voice for utility consumers. Many of the companies we are dealing with in the UK are European and have investments and interests across the globe. They have influence. They provide power and they have power. They are acquiring multi-utility businesses, supplying gas, electricity, water, telephony. Consumers by contrast have enormous potential for influence but negligible central organisation and focus. Some equalising of power has to happen. Consumer bodies have to think in terms of multiplication: of resources, of influence, of action. Consumer representation needs the critical mass of multi-networks with regulators, with other consumer bodies, across borders and across utilities. The need to target resources for maximum impact was a recommendation of a recent British Government report into consumer representation in regulated industries[1]. energywatch has already put in place a research strategy to assess consumer needs using the full range of market research techniques and we are currently bidding, with 14 organisations in Europe, to do major research over the next three years into consumer protection in utility markets. Consumer representation in the utility markets is a European challenge and it should be seen as a particular challenge to utility regulators. One of reasons energywatch was set up was to keep our market regulator focused on consumer issues. We are beginning to see results: Ofgem had taken one enforcement action a year since it was established. This year, with our prompting, it has taken four.

One of the ways we have chosen to strengthen our consumer voice and start to grow multi-networks was to establish a Consumer Action Network (CAN). The prompt came from the Government, which was looking for more efficient use and targeting of the resources of GB's many consumer bodies. The way it is developing will bring greater gains than a consolidation exercise. This is our opportunity to grow a pan-Europe consumer network and we are looking for partners.

The network currently brings together key organisations in the UK involved in helping consumers with complaints or advice. Its purpose is to maximise the use of our resources by:

- exchanging information, experience and ideas about the provision of information and advice and casework handling
- sharing intelligence and research about market developments, consumer trends and companies

---

1   Department of Trade and Industry and Treasury Report, July 2004.

- developing best practice in specific areas of service delivery
- setting up arrangements for pooling resources and the commissioning of joint projects and initiatives.

The possibility of co-operation on policy and lobbying initiatives is not ruled out, but the main emphasis of the network is to promote developments on the practical side, drawing especially on bodies with specific sector responsibilities.

Our view is that consumers in any liberalised market need a strong voice and active protection and that this can only be achieved in any lasting way by dealing with the markets, national or global, with a strategy for collaborative and consumer-focused representation.

A brief history of energywatch

energywatch was formed under the Utilities Act 2000 and opened for business in November 2000. It has a London headquarters and regional offices. It is a Non Departmental Public Body (NDPB) and is independent of Government and Industry although funded through grant aid by the Department of Trade and Industry. Funding is protected under the Utilities Act 2000 and its current budget is 13 million pounds.

energywatch's mission is to be an independent consumer champion, dynamic in developing safe, confident and assertive consumers and committed to improving the services provided to all gas and electricity consumers.

Its duties are to protect and promote the interests of energy consumers. In doing this it must have regard for consumers (present and future) who are of pensionable age, disabled, chronically sick, on low incomes or residing in rural areas.

It has seven work themes:

- delivering effective consumer services
- fostering confident and assertive consumers
- championing the interests of vulnerable consumers
- promoting an effective energy market
- achieving consumer rights through compliance and enforcement
- securing efficient and safe energy networks and supply
- energy consumers and sustainable development.

XI. Podiumsdiskussion

Die britischen Consumer Watchdogs – eine Option für Deutschland?

Teilnehmer:

Allan Asher, Chief Executive Energywatch, Großbritannien

Edward Blades, Department of Trade and Industry (DTI), Großbritannien

Angelika Brunkhorst, MdB

Matthias Kurth, Präsident der Regulierungsbehörde für Telekommunikation und Post

Dr. Klaus Lippold, MdB

Dr. Reinhard Loske, MdB

Michael Müller, MdB

Dr. Franz-Georg Rips, Bundesdirektor Deutscher Mieterbund e.V.

Claude Turmes, MdEP

Moderation:

Prof. Dr. Edda Müller, Vorstand Verbraucherzentrale Bundesverband e.V.

Dokumentation: Anja Dobrodinsky

Motiv und Ziel der Tagung, so eröffnet **Edda Müller** das Podium, ist, von Großbritannien zu lernen. Zu lernen, wie man effektiven Wettbewerb auf regulierten Märkten erreicht und wie man dafür sorgen könne, dass die Energiepreise nicht in den Himmel steigen. Das positive Beispiel der Energieregulierung in Großbritannien untermauert Müller mit folgenden Zahlen: Vor Steuern zahlen Verbraucher dort nur die Hälfte der deutschen Gas- und Strompreise. „Angenommen wir lägen in Deutschland auf dem gleichen Strom- und Gaspreisniveau wie in Großbritannien, allein im Privatkundenbereich hätten wir eine Einsparung von sechs Milliarden Euro beim Strom und fünf Milliarden beim Gas, die zusätzlich in den Konsum fließen könnten." Müller führt an, dass in Deutschland seit der Öffnung der Märkte nur vier Prozent der privaten Haushalte den Stromanbieter gewechselt haben, in Großbritannien beträgt die Wechselquote im Vergleich 50 Prozent. Beim Gas gibt es überhaupt keinen Wettbewerb.

Der Europaabgeordnete **Claude Turmes** lobt die Arbeit des Europäischen Parlaments in Sachen Re-Regulierung des Energiemarktes: „Eine erste EU-Richtlinie brachte 1997 eine Teilöffnung des Marktes, sah gleichzeitig aber fast keine Instrumente der Regulierung vor." Das Europäische Parlament brachte wenig später Regeln in diesen Markt: „Wir haben es fertig gebracht, gegen den erbitterten Widerstand der deutschen Energieversorger und von Wirtschaftsminister Müller seiner Zeit, einen Regulierer für Deutschland vorzuschreiben. Wir wären gern noch weiter gegangen in der Definition seiner Aufgaben." Das EU-Parlament hatte eine Ex-ante-Preisregulierung vorgeschlagen, war dann aber „im EU-Energieministerrat an dem Veto der deutschen und der französischen Regierung gescheitert. Die Lobbyisten von e.on, RWE und EDF (Electricité de France) hatten ganze Arbeit geleistet." Deshalb legte die europäische Richtlinie nur eine Ex-post-Regulierung fest. Nach Turmes kommt man damit aber nicht weiter. Das so genannte *ownership unbundling* fehle. „Es ist eine Illusion, dass der Markt funktionieren kann, solange die Netze und die kommerziellen Aktivitäten in der selben Hand liegen", urteilt Turmes. Der Marktzugang kann so immer behindert werden, und es wäre ein riesiger Regulierungsapparat nötig, um Marktbehinderungen zu verhindern. Als Beispiel nennt Turmes einen Blackout in Teilen von Rheinland-Pfalz und Luxemburg. Eine Analyse hatte ergeben, dass RWE eingespart und Geld von den Netzen weggenommen hatte, um es in Werbung und Marketing zu stecken.

Im Bereich des Verbraucherschutzes plädiert Turmes für einen Perspektivenwechsel weg von *Consumer protection* hin zu *Consumer empowerment*. Aus seiner Sicht müssen dabei folgende Fragen geklärt werden: „Wie bringen wir die Einzelkunden, die ja in Konkurrenz zu den großen Industriekunden stehen, in eine Position, in der sie Macht am Markt haben? Wie können wir die Kleinkunden wieder bündeln?" Dazu verweist er auf das positive Beispiel von Newcastle in England. Die Stadt ging für ihre Bürger in die Verhandlungen und handelte so einen besseren Energiepreis heraus als die einzelnen Kunden. Auch mache eine Liberalisierung nur Sinn, so Turmes weiter, wenn man eine Wahl über die Qualität und Herkunft seines Stromes habe. Daher sei die Kennzeichnung des Stroms so wichtig. Nur über die Kennzeichnung kann der Kunde erfahren, aus welchen Energiequellen sein Strom kommt.

Den deutschen Energiemarkt vergleicht Turmes mit einer Bananenrepublik: „Ich kann nicht verstehen, warum so lange in der Öffentlichkeit diesem Spiel zugeschaut wurde und ich freue mich, dass sich seit drei, vier Wochen der Wind dreht. Das deutsche Wirtschaftsministerium hat die Interessen der Versorger in Brüssel bislang überrepräsentiert." Statt eines fairen Wettbewerbs gäbe es in Deutschland riesige Konzentrationen und erst die Anfänge einer Regulierungsbehörde. Die Verbraucherverbände müssen sich in Zukunft vor allem für mehr Wettbewerb einsetzen, regt er an.

Edward Blades vom Britischen Department of Trade and Industry erläutert den Prozess der in Großbritannien zur Einrichtung von Regulierungsbehörden und *watchdogs* geführt hat: „Die Regierung erließ ein Gesetz, das uns das Recht gab zu privatisieren und sowohl eine Regulierungsbehörde als auch eine Verbrauchervertretung einzurichten." Somit waren zwei der drei Grundsäulen, neben Regulierung und Verbraucherrepräsentanz ist das der Wettbewerb, bereits gesichert. Jede der Liberalisierungsmaßnahmen musste dem Parlament vorgelegt werden. Blades erläutert, dass es die *Watchdogs* zum Teil bereits seit 20 Jahren gibt, sie wiederholt reformiert wurden und heute gute Arbeit leisten. „Sie verstehen die Bedürfnisse der Verbraucher und übersetzen sie in Aufgaben für den Regulierer, die Unternehmen und die Regierung", so Blades. Für die Zukunft schlägt er vor, die verschiedenen *Watchdogs* unter einem Dach zusammenbringen, um sie noch stärker und effektiver zu machen. Den gesetzlichen Auftrag der *Watchdogs* bestimmt Blades wie folgt: „Sie müssen dem Verbraucher Informationen zur Verfügung stellen." Die *Watchdogs* in Großbritannien finanzieren sich durch Lizenzgebühren, welche die Firmen an die Regulierungsbehörden zahlen. So werden die Wirtschaftsbereiche, die Gegenstand der Regulierung sind, an den Kosten beteiligt. Steuermittel werden daher nicht benötigt.

Edda Müller fasst die Situation in Deutschland zusammen: „Wir brauchen einen starken Ansprechpartner gegenüber der Regulierungsbehörde, ein eigenes Beschwerdemanagement in den Unternehmen und Schlichtungsinstanzen, wenn Probleme von den Unternehmen nicht zufriedenstellend gelöst werden. In Deutschland haben wir die Strukturen für einen solchen Mechanismus. Was uns fehlt, ist ein klarer gesetzlicher Auftrag, ein klarer rechtlicher Rahmen und die Finanzierung", kommentiert sie.

Michael Müller unterstreicht für die SPD-Bundestagsfraktion die Vorteile einer nachfrageorientierten Sichtweise: „Verbraucherschutz ist die eine Seite, noch wichtiger ist allerdings die Verbraucherpolitik." Die Nachfrageseite, vor allem die Stärkung der Nachfrage, sind bisher viel zu wenig beachtet worden. Sie gehört aber genauso zu einer leistungsfähigen, innovativen Marktwirtschaft. Dies sei aber der Schlüssel für einen funktionierenden Wettbewerb. „Wir müssen in der Energiepolitik über den Schutzgedanken weit hinausgehen", fordert Müller, „zu einer funktionierenden Marktwirtschaft gehören selbstbewusste Akteure, die fähig sind, Fehlentwicklungen zu benennen und zu korrigieren." Entscheidend sind mehr Transparenz und mehr Klarheit. Es reicht nicht aus, nur über Regulierung nachzudenken. Der Glaube an die billige Energie der Zukunft ist ein Irrglaube, denn das Energiesystem der Welt sei nach Müller für nur eine Milliarde Menschen konzipiert. Und selbst das schafft gewaltige ökologische Probleme. „Jetzt aber muss dieses System für drei bis vier Milliarden Menschen ausreichen. Deshalb halte ich es für eine schlichte Illusion zu glauben, dass wir diese Probleme mit einer reinen Preisregulierung in den Griff kriegen", urteilt er. Ein neues Verständnis von Energiepolitik muss entwickelt werden, weil effiziente Kraftwerke allein nicht ausreichen. Müller regt einen Paradigmenwechsel vom Schutz- zum Gestaltungsgedanken an. Dazu gehört, für eine dauerhafte Finanzierung nicht nur den Staat zur Kasse zu bitten. Außerdem müssen die Interessen der Verbraucher auch dort institutionell verankert werden, wo die Preisbildung stattfindet.

Einen wettbewerbsorientierten Ansatz liefert **Klaus Lippold**, Mitglied der CDU-Bundestagsfraktion: „Wir haben überall da einen guten Verbraucherschutz, wo es Wettbewerb gibt", hebt er hervor. Deshalb gelte es, den Wettbewerb zu stärken, nicht nur zwischen Unternehmen, sondern auch zwischen den Energieformen. „Ein breiter Energiemix ohne Ausschluss einzelner Energiearten ist wichtig", so Lippold weiter. Er plädiert dafür, diesen Wettbewerb nicht nur in Deutschland zu organisieren, sondern auch europaweit „dort nachzubohren, wo nicht liberalisiert wurde, wie zum Beispiel in Frankreich bei der EDF." Auch hat man sich in letzter Zeit zu wenig um die Themen „Energieeinsparung" und „Energieeffizienzsteigerung" gekümmert. Lippold verweist auf einen Vorschlag der unionsgeführten Länder im Bundesrat, eine Ex-ante-Lösung mit schlanker Bürokratie zu finden. „Damit wäre ein Vorabdenken bei den Unternehmen verbunden" und „es träte ein disziplinierender Effekt ein", begründet er.

„Wenn wir über Netzregulierung reden, brauchen wir auch Transparenz bei der Vergabe und Veröffentlichung von Gutachten durch die Bundesregierung", so Lippold weiter. Er übt Kritik an der Bundesregierung, die eine bereits vorliegende DENA-Studie zu diesem Thema nicht veröffentlicht. „Es kann sein, dass die Ergebnisse dieser Studie der Bundesregierung nicht bequem genug sind, aber wir haben Anspruch auf Faktenkenntnis."

Die britischen *Watchdogs* sieht Lippold als Anregung, über die Stärkung der Beteiligung der Verbraucher nachzudenken. Er bezweifelt, dass ein Systemwechsel im englischen Sinne den deutschen Verbrauchern zugute kommt. „In Großbritannien wird ja auch über Effizienzsteigerung nachgedacht. Wir werden uns also noch mal über die Frage Finanzierung und Beteiligung unterhalten müssen", fasst er zusammen.

Reinhard Loske, Mitglied der Bundestagsfraktion von Bündnis 90/Die Grünen, rät dazu, sich den Status quo in Sachen Energieregulierung vor Augen zu führen: „In den Landeswirtschaftsministerien gibt es meist nur ein Referat mit zwei bis drei Referenten, die sich mit der Genehmigung der Energie-Tarife beschäftigen." Aufgrund dieser Unterbesetzung sind die Länder in der Vergangenheit nicht besonders scharf vorgegangen. Jetzt eine Mischzuständigkeit zwischen der Regulierungsbehörde und den Ländern vorzuschlagen, hält er daher für „keine gute Idee, da machen wir auf gar keinen Fall mit." Sinnvoller sei es, diese Arbeit ganz in die Hand der Wettbewerbsbehörde zu legen und diese mit einem Instrumentarium auszustatten, das sie in die Lage versetzt, ihrer Tarifaufsicht auch gerecht zu werden. „Ich bin für eine Ex-ante-Regulierung, sofort oder schrittweise", so Loske weiter. Am allerwichtigsten ist im Moment aber, dass das Gesetz schnell in Kraft tritt. „Der Wind hat sich gedreht in den letzten Wochen. Jetzt sind alle der Meinung, man müsse den Wettbewerb durch eine funktionierende Wettbewerbsaufsicht vorantreiben. Jetzt ist Druck im Kessel", fügt er hinzu.

Sich selbst bezeichnet Loske als „Fan des *Watchdog*-Modells". In der SPD-Fraktion herrscht eine große Aufgeschlossenheit, man will die Verbraucherrechte stärken. Über die Finanzierungsmechanismen und die Form der Institutionalisierung müsse man reden. Außerdem weist Loske auf die lange Tradition des Korporatismus in Deutschland hin: „Der große Staat trifft mit der großen Industrie große Absprachen, gelegentlich unter Beteiligung der großen Gewerkschaften, aber oft zu Lasten Dritter." Jetzt wird diese Praxis auf dem Energiemarkt durch eine Wettbewerbsaufsicht abgelöst. Da ist es klar, dass es zu Reibungen kommt. „Aber wir können es uns nicht mehr leisten, dass in so erheblichem Umfang Monopolgewinne abgeschöpft werden", betont er. Er begrüßt den Druck von europäischer Seite auf Deutschland, weil der alte deutsche Korporatismus gesprengt werden müsse.

Angelika Brunkhorst vertritt den Standpunkt der FDP-Bundestagsfraktion in Sachen Energieregulierung: „Wir möchten ja gerade durch den neuen Ordnungsrahmen mehr Wettbewerb in den Netzen schaffen", hebt sie hervor. Sie befürwortet eine möglichst leistungsstarke Regulierungsbehörde. Nach Brunkhorst bedeutet das aber nicht, dass der Staat die Preise festsetzen soll, sondern die Behörde soll bei Verstößen gegen die Wettbewerbsfairness in den Markt eingreifen können.

„Außerdem meinen wir, dass es insbesondere im Bereich der Netze Einsparpotentiale gibt, die an den Verbraucher weitergegeben werden können", führt sie aus. Die Diskussion hat zwei Seiten: Einerseits ist der Strompreis mittlerweile fast ein „Killerfaktor für das Verbraucherbudget" geworden, so Brunkhorst. „Da muss sich etwas tun, damit wir auch weiterhin vom Standort her wettbewerbsfähig sind", fordert sie. Andererseits wünscht sich die FDP, dass die Regulierungsbehörde überhaupt erst einmal mit ihrer Arbeit beginnt. Das Modell der *Consumer Watchdogs* bezeichnet Brunkhorst als sympathisch, fügt aber hinzu, dass man in einem ersten Schritt „das Ganze nicht überfrachten, sondern zuerst die Regulierungsbehörde für Telekommunikation und Post zur Arbeit kommen lassen soll." Die Verbraucherverbände seien bereits gut vernetzt und haben heute schon Fachleute, die sich mit Energiepolitik beschäftigen. „Ich fühle mich als Verbraucher nicht so wehrlos ausgeliefert, wie das hier teilweise anklang", bemerkte sie. Wenn tatsächlich mehr Aufsicht notwendig oder die Regulierungsbehörde für Telekommunikation und Post überfordert wäre, dann kann man private Firmen mit der Beobachtung des Energiemarktes beauftragen. Die FDP hat immer Bedenken, „wenn es darum geht, zu institutionalisieren und bestehende Verbände, die ja auch gut funktionieren, aufzublähen". Frau Brunkhorst regt an, dass sich die Verbraucherorganisationen „auf das konzentrieren, was sie schon geschaffen haben."

Franz-Georg Rips vom Deutschen Mieterbund weist auf die „zweite Miete", die Energie- oder Betriebskosten hin, die „heute bereits ein Drittel bis die Hälfte der gesamten Wohnkosten betragen." Transparenz gäbe es auf dem deutschen Wohnungsmarkt nicht. Zum energetischen Zustand von Gebäuden fehle jede systematische Darstellung. Er plädiert dafür, den von der DENA vorgeschlagenen Gebäudepass bundeseinheitlich einzuführen: „Damit hätten wir ein Transparenzinstrument, das den energetischen Zustand von Wohnungen und Gebäuden vergleichbar macht." An einem Beispiel veranschaulicht er das Thema Energiepreise: „Wenn sich die Energiekosten erhöhen, dann heißt das für einen Arbeitslosengeld-II-Empfänger, dass er die gesamte Mehrbelastung im Bereich der Stromkosten selbst tragen muss." Damit wird an die Grenzen der Belastbarkeit gegangen. Rips appelliert, „diese historische Situation zu nutzen", in der das Energiewirtschaftsgesetz verabschiedet wird. Er spricht sich für eine Ex-ante-Regulierung aus, die nicht nur Missbrauchskontrolle betreibt, denn die vorhandenen Rechtsinstrumente in Deutschland seien unwirksam. Das Kartellrecht eignet sich nicht dafür, die Missbräuche der natürlichen Monopolisten zu bekämpfen.

Anja Dobrodinsky

Anschließend beschreibt **Allan Asher** die Beziehung zwischen *Energywatch* und der britischen Regulierungsbehörde: „Wir haben komplementäre Aufgaben. Wir tun weder dasselbe, noch arbeiten wir in entgegengesetzten Richtungen. Das bedeutet aber nicht, dass wir immer einer Meinung sind." Regulierer und *Energywatch* arbeiten auf vielerlei Ebenen zusammen, so Asher. Der *Watchdog* ermutigt die Verbraucher, den Markt mit ihrer Kaufkraft zu beeinflussen und zum Beispiel den Energieversorger zu wechseln. Im Gegenzug kann der Regulierer Energieunternehmen Strafgebühren von bis zu zehn Prozent ihres Umsatzes auferlegen, wenn diese die Lizenz-Regeln brechen. Allerdings, so Asher, ist der Regulierer bei der Beweisführung von Verstößen nicht in der besten Position. Andererseits hat seine Organisation täglich Kontakt mit Hunderten von Verbrauchern, im Jahr sind es sogar eine Million Verbraucher. Energywatch bündelt die Beschwerden und legt sie dem Regulierer vor, der dann reagieren kann.

In anderen Bereichen bezeichnet Asher die Beziehung zwischen der britischen Regulierungsbehörde und Energywatch als „etwas angespannter", besonders in ökonomischen Fragen der Regulierung. Auch in diesem Bereich, fordert Asher, die *Watchdogs* mit einzubeziehen: „Im Moment gibt es in Großbritannien sechs Energieversorger, die den gesamten Markt kontrollieren. Die beschäftigen die sechs teuersten Beraterfirmen, die sechs teuersten Public Relations-Firmen und bieten den Regulierern die sechs eindrucksvollsten Sitzplätze beim Fußball an." Asher macht auf die Diskrepanz bei der Ausstattung aufmerksam. Die Regulierungsbehörde hat nur 300 Mitarbeiter, die Firmen hingegen verfügen über Ressourcen von mehreren zehn Milliarden Euro. Asher sieht die *Watchdogs* als „Floh im Ohr des Regulierers, ... der ihn daran erinnert, dass es auch Verbraucherinteressen gibt."

Matthias Kurth, Präsident der Regulierungsbehörde für Telekommunikation und Post, merkt an, dass die neue Regulierungsbehörde für den Energiemarkt in Deutschland nur auf einen Mitarbeiterstab von 60 zurückgreifen kann. „Schon diese Zahl wird hierzulande als viel zu bürokratisch angesehen", fügt er hinzu. Die Behörde könne ihre Aufgaben nur erfüllen, wenn sie von allen Marktteilnehmern Anregungen aufnimmt. Deshalb fordert er grundsätzlich jeden Beteiligten auf, Stellung zu nehmen. Auch kritische Stimmen seien erwünscht. Allerdings gibt es auch in Großbritannien nicht in jedem Bereich einen *Watchdog*, zum Beispiel im Bereich Telekommunikation. Auch dort werden die Vor- und Nachteile diskutiert. Ihm ist wichtig, dass keine doppelte Arbeit geleistet wird und es eine klare Aufgabenteilung gibt. Die Regulierungsbehörde für Telekommunikation und Post lege großen Wert auf die Vertretung der Verbraucherinteressen. Sie berät nicht nur, sondern kann auch handeln, betont Kurth. „Wenn sich zum Beispiel jemand über eine betrügerische Aktion im Telefonnetz beklagt und sagt, ich bin Opfer eines Dialers geworden, dann kann unsere Behörde innerhalb einer Woche die Abschaltung einer Nummer anordnen. Es ist manchmal ganz gut, wenn der, der auch handeln kann, direkt im Kontakt mit Verbrauchern steht." Diese Kompetenz soll nach Kurth nicht abgegeben werden. Er stimmt seinen Vorrednern zu, dass ein funktionierender Wettbewerb auch das beste für die Verbraucher sei. Allerdings weist er dabei auch auf einen Konflikt hin: „Wann immer die Regulierungsbehörde im Hinblick auf die Wettbewerbsförderung höhere Preise verlangt, reagieren die Verbraucher verständnislos; auch wenn Firmen versuchen, Wettbewerber mit Dumpingpreisen vom Markt zu fegen." Mit Blick auf die Preisregulierung sagt Kurth: „Ich finde es etwas verwunderlich, dass man sich so sehr über *ex ante und ex post* streitet. Diese Diskussion bringt nichts, wenn den Regulierern das entsprechende Instrumentarium fehlt." In Einzelprüfverfahren könne man sich sehr schnell verlieren.

Aus dem Publikum greift **Karl-Heinz Neumann** vom Wissenschaftlichen Institut für Kommunikationsdienste ein deutsches Phänomen auf: „In Großbritannien haben schon 50 Prozent aller Verbraucher den Stromanbieter gewechselt, in Deutschland sind es nur vier Prozent". Interessant sei, welche Unterschiede zwischen dem Verbraucherverhalten in Deutschland und England bestehen und ob die Angebots- und Regulierungsumstände die Ursache für das mangelnde Wechselverhalten der Verbraucher sind. **Edward Blades** antwortet mit Verweis auf die Trägheit der Verbraucher. Es ist eben sehr bequem, so Blades, einfach alles beim alten zu belassen: „In den Anfängen der Marktliberalisierung waren wir immer wieder enttäuscht über die geringe Zahl von Verbrauchern, die den Stromanbieter wechselten". Neben der Trägheit sei es für viele Verbraucher auch wenig verlockend, die Belastung eines Wechsels auf sich zu nehmen, wenn am Ende keine große Ersparnis winkt. „Dies änderte sich, als die Stromanbieter begannen, auch Gas zu verkaufen und umgekehrt", erläutert Blades. Die Regulierungsbehörde in Großbritannien bemüht sich, die Verbraucher mit Informationen zu versorgen, wie durch einem Anbieterwechsel Geld gespart werden kann. Diese Bemühungen dauern an und helfen dem Kunden, den Markt zu verstehen.

Allan Asher ergänzt: „Ich bin nicht dafür, dem Opfer die Schuld zu geben, indem man fragt, warum sich das Verbraucherverhalten nicht ändert." Viel wichtiger sei die Frage nach den Strukturen oder Handlungsweisen der Industrie, die eine Veränderung verhindern. „Die oberste Theorie für wettbewerbsfähige Märkte ist", so Asher weiter, „dass ein Händler, der sich sicher ist, das bessere Produkt zu haben, dieses auch aggressiv anbietet." Dies ist in Deutschland nicht der Fall, denn vielen Unternehmen ist das schlicht und einfach egal. „Der Markt funktioniert einfach nicht", stellt Asher fest. Angelika Brunkhorst weist auf die Ängste der Verbraucher hin: „Ich habe den Eindruck, dass der Verbraucher, gerade wenn es um einen Wechsel des Energieversorgungsunternehmens geht, doch sehr viele Ängste hat, weil er sich fragt, wenn ich jetzt kündige, schalten die mir den Strom sofort ab?" Wichtig sei es, die Verbraucher zu bestärken, sich verschiedene Angebote einzuholen, so wie das bei jeder handwerklichen Leistung üblich ist. „Der Verbraucher muss seine Macht erkennen", fügt sie hinzu, „in Deutschland sind wir in dieser Hinsicht vielleicht ein bisschen phlegmatisch."

Verbraucherinteressen in der Energiepolitik dürfen nicht nur „billig, billig, billig" bedeuten, wirft **Reinhard Loske** in die Diskussion ein. Außerdem soll der Anbieterwechsel vereinfacht werden. **Michael Müller** schließt sich dem Statement von Reinhard Loske an. Er fordert die Industrieländer auf, zu anderen energiepolitischen Strategien als nur „billig, billig, billig" zu kommen. Aus drei Gründen wäre es bei uns schwieriger zu wechseln. Erstens entstehen bei einem Wechsel hohe Kosten für Ablesegeräte und Zähler; zweitens haben viele Verbraucher Angst vor der Übergangsphase und drittens gibt es Kunden, die bestimmte Stromarten einfach nicht wollen, argumentiert Müller. Die Bauernfängerei von Yello Strom hat zum Glück nicht funktioniert, bemerkt er. Und zum Streit *ex ante* versus *ex post* stellt er fest: „Was das Gesetz und die Regulierung angeht, glaube ich, dass *ex ante* leichter ist, aber ich würde daraus kein Dogma, keinen Prinzipienstreit machen."

Zum Schluss der Podiumsdiskussion bemerkt **Claude Turmes** einen Wechsel in der Strategie der Europäischen Kommission: „Bis vor wenigen Wochen hat man geglaubt, dass dieser Markt funktionieren würde. Aber wir sind von staatlichen Monopolen zu privaten Oligopolen übergegangen. Seit wenigen Wochen ist die Kommission plötzlich der Meinung, dass infrastrukturgebundene Märkte anders funktionieren und die Marktkonzentration deshalb auch anders angegangen werden muss." Turmes berichtet von Gesprächen über eine dritte Liberalisierungsrichtlinie, die 2005/2006 auf den Weg gebracht werden soll. In diese Richtlinie, so Turmes, fließen dann auch wirksame Instrumente ein, wie *Electricity release*, *Divestment*, und *Ownership unbundling*. Turmes spricht auch die Diskrepanzen zwischen Brüssel und der Bundesregierung an: „Wir bearbeiten im Parlament gerade in zweiter Lesung eine Richtlinie über den Zugang zu den Gasnetzen. Die Bundesregierung macht dieses Instrument unter dem Druck von e.on/Ruhrgas wieder intransparent und verhindert den Zugang." Auch in punkto Energieeffizienz folgt Berlin nicht den europäischen Maßgaben: „Wir haben eine Richtlinie zur Energieeffizienz auf dem Tisch, denn ein Markt nur für Kilowattstunden macht keinen Sinn. Wir brauchen einen Markt für Energiedienstleistungen. Die deutsche Bundesregierung ist aber gegen diese Richtlinie. Sie vertritt in Brüssel die Privatinteressen von drei oder vier Konzernen und nicht das Allgemeininteresse", stellt er dar. Die Energie-Bananenrepublik Deutschland könne nur abgeschafft werden, wenn klar zwischen den Interessen der Versorgungsunternehmen und den allgemeinen Interessen unterschieden werde.

Zweiter Abschnitt

Consumer Representation in Regulated Industries

A report by the Department of Trade and Industry and HM Treasury, July 2004

Executive Summary

1. In September 2003, the DTI and HM Treasury began a joint study into consumer representation in regulated markets. The aim was to assess the efficiency and effectiveness of the existing sectoral consumer bodies, sharing best practice and developing a set of recommendations to further enhance the effectiveness of consumer bodies in the medium term. This report presents the findings of the study. It also sets out a possible model for future consumer representation in regulated markets.

2. The study has provided valuable insight into the policy framework for consumer representation by reviewing arrangements across a number of sectors. This report focuses on consumer representation in the utility sectors, air transport, and financial services. However, the report also has regard to the broader consumer environment taking account of the role played by Consumers Association and the National Consumer Council, and drawing on the experience of the Rail Passenger Council, Alternative Dispute Resolution mechanisms in the communications sector such as Otelo, and the Financial Ombudsman Service.

3. The report's recommendations are underpinned by a vision of strategic and proactive consumer bodies, offering good value for money for the customer, and operating within a regulatory system that works well for all consumers. Achieving this vision will depend on a number of key factors:
   - Each of the sectoral consumer bodies needs to become more strategic and proactive in its approach to consumer representation.
   - The consumer bodies must demonstrate value for money; since customers or taxpayers ultimately provide their funding. In some sectors, there will be a need to address:
     - Regional representation: is it cost effective and does it add value for customers?

- Complaints handling: it must meet the needs of consumers, but are there clear incentives on companies to minimise complaints by delivering a high-quality service?
- The whole regulatory framework must work well for all consumers: Consumer bodies, regulators, companies and Government need to work together to ensure that consumers get a good deal in regulated markets.

4. The report recognises the significant achievements of the sectoral consumer bodies to date. Energywatch and Postwatch, in particular, have managed the high levels of consumer complaints they received, and they earn generally positive feedback about their service. All of the bodies can exhibit positive achievements on their effects on market behaviour or regulatory decisions. Very many examples of good practice set out in the report are derived from the innovations made by the consumer bodies themselves.

5. Following this successful start-up phase, there are some issues emerging which could be addressed by the consumer bodies:

- Consumer bodies may become unduly reactive, responding to the regulator's agenda or work programme. There is scope for greater focus on issues which will affect consumers in the future, or which are not at present a high priority for the regulator.
- Resources devoted to sectoral consumer representation are spread across six organisations and twenty-seven regional offices[1]. This makes it difficult to achieve economies of scale, and to develop a critical mass to tackle project and programme management. This can also raise problems in ensuring co-ordination and consistency of approach.
- Consumer bodies may target issues which are easiest to measure, instead of focusing on the points which have greatest impact on consumers. Some consumer bodies do not have processes in place to measure the impact of their activities.

6. There are also some issues that are more apparent in markets where there are independent statutory consumer bodies.

- Consumer bodies may expend too much resource on dealing with the effects of consumer dissatisfaction in the form of complaints instead of addressing the underlying causes of market failure. This reduces the incen-

---

1 This includes energywatch, Postwatch, WaterVoice, Financial Services Consumer Panel, OFCOM Consumer Panel and the Air Transport Users Council. Both consumer panels use facilities when necessary at their regulators premises and therefore do not have fixed offices.

tives on the companies involved to resolve consumer problems themselves.
- A confrontational relationship can arise between the regulator and the consumer body. An excessively adversarial stance can give rise to increased costs and delays, and risks undermining the credibility of the regulator.

7. This report concludes that the recommendations on best practice for sectoral consumer bodies point toward a new framework for sectoral consumer representation, where:
   - suppliers of services are strongly incentivised to provide higher standards of customer care and specifically to deal effectively with consumer complaints;
   - the number of different contact points for information and advice can be simplified, to the benefit of consumers in terms of clarity and ease of use; and
   - the consumer representation and advocacy functions can be tackled from a position of greater strength and a broader understanding of consumer needs.

8. In order to achieve this, the framework should comprise:
   - Consumer Direct handling enquiries;
   - suppliers dealing effectively with consumer complaints;
   - complaints not resolved between the customer and supplier being handled by alternative dispute resolution bodies such as ombudsmen;
   - regional representation being maintained where necessary; and
   - sectoral bodies coming together to form a single National Utilities Consumer Council, providing a more effective, strategic voice for utility consumers.

9. In this report it is assumed that a National Utilities Consumer Council would cover traditional utilities. However, the exact remit and scope of this new body should not be fixed and should remain sufficiently flexible to expand or modify its remit to respond to changing demands.

10. Furthermore, the full realisation of this model for sectoral consumer representation would depend on a number of factors, including the successful roll-out of Consumer Direct and on further work and analysis being undertaken on other aspects of the package. It is important that this proposal should be considered by all interested parties. Consequently, views are being sought on the proposal as part of a wider public consultation that is being undertaken by the Department for Trade and Industry in July 2004.

11. The Department for Trade and Industry (DTI) and HM Treasury (HMT) will continue to work with the consumer bodies to take forward the key findings in this report.

12. There are other reports being published by Government which are relevant to the issues addressed in this project report. The National Audit Office (NAO) has undertaken its own separate report on energywatch and Postwatch, and they plan to publish a report in September.

13. The NAO has considered how the two bodies have determined their priorities; what they have achieved; and the costs incurred. In order to minimise the burden on participating bodies, NAO, HM Treasury and the DTI jointly commissioned PricewaterhouseCoopers (PwC) to assess the efficiency and effectiveness of energywatch and Postwatch against similar bodies, and that report will be published alongside the NAO report. The PwC report has been utilised to help develop both this report and the NAO report.

14. The Department for Constitutional Affairs will very soon be publishing a White Paper entitled "Transforming Public Services: Complaints, Redress and Tribunals", which describes the Government's plans to take forward the proposals for tribunals reform in Sir Andrew Leggatt's report "Tribunals for Users – One System, One Service".

1. Introduction

1.1 Consumer policy has been a high priority for this Government. In July 1999 the Government published its Consumer White Paper, „Modern markets: confident consumers" which set out a new agenda for consumer policy. It stated, "Confident consumers, making informed decisions in modern, competitive markets, promote the development of innovative and good value products. And better performance in business in turn benefits consumers"[2]. To deliver this mission statement, the Government set a new agenda to:

- promote open and competitive markets;
- provide people with the skills, knowledge and information they need to become demanding consumers; and
- encourage responsible businesses to follow good practice.

---

[2] 'Modern markets: Confident consumers' – http://www.dti.gov.uk/consumer/whitepaper/overview.htm.

1.2 The Government is also currently reviewing the UK consumer framework, and will publish a consultation paper in July 2004 drawing on the comparative benchmarking report published in October 2003[3].

1.3 Although the Consumer White Paper did not cover consumers' experiences in regulated markets in detail, the desired outcomes in regulated markets are much the same as elsewhere in the economy: more demanding consumers taking opportunities to switch in competitive situations, better functioning markets, sharper incentives on regulated companies, and high levels of trust between suppliers and consumers.

1.4 The Utilities Review (1998) set out the objective of securing a fair deal for all consumers – especially disadvantaged groups – in using the essential services that utilities provide. The subsequent White Paper[4] confirmed the Government's intention to establish consumer councils for the utilities on an independent statutory basis. This was an important part of the agenda to ensure that the regulatory regime served the needs of consumers. The Government proposed that these utility consumer bodies should:

- articulate a strategic, independent view of the consumer interest to Government, Parliament and the media;
- work constructively with the utility companies to reduce the causes of consumer complaints, but also provide "one stop shops" for consumer complaints that were not resolved by the utilities;
- help regulators in developing policy that takes account of consumer needs and interests;
- publish information and advice to assist consumers in getting a fair deal from the utilities companies; and
- monitor and report on the impact of change on the disadvantaged – competition will have failed if it does not bring benefits for all.

1.5 Increasing competition in many of the utility sectors has provided significant benefits for many consumers. In energy and telecommunications markets, consumers have a choice from an increasing number of suppliers and an array of different tariffs. In this phase of market development, strong consumer bodies can play an important role in articulating the consumer interest, ensuring that suppliers take their responsibilities to customers seriously and

---

[3] Comparative Report on Consumer Policy Regimes – http://www.dti.gov.uk/ccp/topics1/pdf1/benchmain.pdf.
[4] A Fair deal for consumers: Modernising the Framework for Utility Regulation : http://www.dti.gov.uk/urt/gas_elec.pdf.

providing the high quality information and advice needed for consumers to take full advantage of competitive markets and to shop around to get the best deals available.

1.6 Influential consumer councils and well-informed consumers therefore have a vital transitional role to play in newly competitive markets in improving standards, encouraging switching and lowering prices. The need for effective consumer representation is equally strong, if not stronger, in those markets in which customers do not have a choice of supplier or where competition is restricted.

1.7 Beyond the utility markets of energy, water, fixed-line telecommunications and postal services, there are a number of other regulated markets where consumer representation is also important. Regulation of specific markets arises as a response to market failure and risks to consumer welfare, such as information shortfalls and restricted competition. In all regulated markets, protecting and promoting consumer interests needs to be a principal objective. Consumer representative bodies and panels have an important role to play in this.

1.8 Six years on from the Utilities Review, and three years from the creation of independent statutory consumer bodies in energy and postal services, consumer representation is now a substantial feature of the regulatory landscape. In 2002/03, the five main sectoral consumer bodies[5] spent just under £25million, employing over 800 staff and representatives, based in 27 offices across the UK. Between them these bodies handled 164,000 complaints in 2002/03 and over 115,000 enquiries[6].

1.9 This report seeks to take stock of progress since the Utilities Review. Its objective is to assess the efficiency and effectiveness of consumer representation in regulated markets, sharing best practice and developing a set of recommendations to further enhance the effectiveness of consumer bodies in the medium term. It also proposes a new model for sectoral consumer representation for the future.

1.10 The scope of this report is drawn wider than the utilities. Some of its findings and recommendations are also addressed to consumer bodies in air trans-

---

[5] Energywatch, Postwatch, WaterVoice, FSA Consumer Panel and Air Transport Users Council. Figures exclude OFCOM consumer panel as it was only established in 2004 and the Rail Passengers Council – see para 1.11.

[6] Source: PricewaterhouseCoopers benchmarking study note that there is not consistency between how consumer bodies classify enquiries and complaints.

A report by the Department of Trade and Industry and HM Treasury

port and financial services. However, it also has regard to the broader consumer environment by taking into account the role played by Consumers Association and the National Consumer Council. It draws on the experience of the Financial Ombudsman Service and the Rail Passenger Council and Alternative Dispute Resolution mechanisms in the communications sector, such as Otelo.

1.11 The Government is currently engaged in a wide-ranging review of the rail industry, including consideration of the structural and organisation changes needed for the railways to operate more effectively for customers.[7] Consumer representation in the rail sector needs to be viewed in this wider context and so falls outside the scope of this report and its recommendations. The project team wishes to ackowledge, with thanks, the significant input made to this project by the Rail Passengers Council, the Office of the Rail Regulator, and the Strategic Rail Authority. The Rail Passengers Council gave generously of their time, and we were able to draw on their experience and processes to find examples of best practice, which influenceds the final recommendations in this report.

Figure 1: Scope

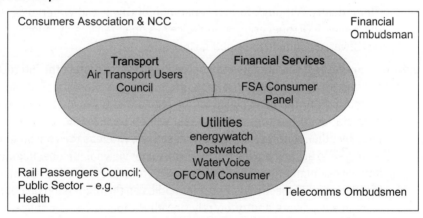

---

[7] Alistair Darling made a statement to the House on Monday 19 January announcing a review of the rail industry which will look at progress being made with the increased investment in the railways; the structural and organisation changes needed so the railways can operate more effectively for its customers, with clear lines of accountability and responsibility, including the regulation of safety. The review rules out as little as possible so as to come up with the best solution. The principles for the review are that: railways must operate in the public interest; maintain commitment to public and private partnership; and maintain commitment to independent economic regulation. The review is being undertaken within Government (though consultants have been brought in to assist) and is drawing on the views of the industry. Its conclusions will be announced in Summer 2004.

1.12 The project has drawn on desk research and stakeholder interviews, as well as an externally commissioned benchmarking study by Pricewaterhouse-Coopers (PWC). This study, which was jointly funded by the National Audit Office and the Department of Trade and Industry, focussed primarily on energywatch and Postwatch, but also drew comparisons with a range of organisations, including sectoral and general consumer bodies. A 'Friends Group' of stakeholders drawn from consumer groups, regulated markets, the regulators and academia met twice during the project to provide strategic direction and feedback on emerging conclusions. The project team is extremely grateful to all those who contributed their time, wisdom and energy.

2. Consumer representation today

2.1 The Utilities Review and subsequent reforms put consumer interests at the heart of utilities regulation. Regulators were given a primary objective to further the interests of consumers; greater emphasis was placed on promoting competition; and statutory consumer bodies – such as energywatch and Postwatch – were established to represent consumer interests in those sectors. As a result of the Water Act (2003), a similar body is being set up in the water industry. Although formal separation of Ofwat and WaterVoice is not expected until October 2005, WaterVoice has operated largely independently from Ofwat, the industry regulator, since 2000.

2.2 In many cases it is a primary duty of the Regulator to protect the interests of consumers[8]. Where this is the case, protecting the interests of consumers becomes an overriding objective for the regulators. However, the regulators' interpretation of the consumer interest will on occasion need to be conditioned by other statutory duties and objectives, whereas the consumer bodies are free to act and advise from the consumer viewpoint alone. Regulators often have a number of enforcement powers to help them achieve their statutory duties and objectives. Consumer bodies on the other hand do not have enforcement powers and often rely on other tools such as publication of comparative information.

---

[8] The regulators for gas and electricity, water (from 2005), telecommunications and rail have objectives to (broadly) promote or protect the interests of consumers. The Postal Services Commission has a primary duty to ensure the provision of a universal postal service. Subject to this primary duty, Postcomm is required to promote effective competition. The Financial Services Authority has regulatory objectives to maintain confidence in the financial system; to promote public understanding of the financial system; to secure the appropriate degree of protection for consumers; and reduce financial crime, in that order.

2.3 Different statutory arrangements apply in other regulated markets. The Financial Services and Markets Act 2000 and the Communications Act 2003 set up the Financial Services Consumer Panel and the OFCOM Consumer Panel respectively. These panels are different in nature to the statutory bodies established in postal and energy markets. They do not handle customer complaints, which are addressed through Ombudsman or Alternative Dispute Resolution schemes. They also are more closely connected to the regulator, and play an advisory role. However, in practice, both FSA and Ofcom have encouraged their consumer panels to operate with a high degree of autonomy, and their independence enjoys considerable protection. Arrangements for consumer representation in the transport sector have not undergone significant statutory change in recent years.

2.4 Consumer representation in regulated markets now has a higher profile and is better resourced than in 1998. Although each of the consumer bodies differs in its approach and practice, they each have an important role in delivering the Government's objectives for consumer policy and regulation. Alongside this, most consumer bodies engage with companies and handle consumer complaints. All, to varying degrees, undertake research to further their understanding of consumer needs and behaviour in their respective markets.

The economic rationale for consumer representation

2.5 Underpinning the policy decisions that emerged from the Utilities Review, there is an economic reality that reinforces the need for consumer representation in each of these regulated markets. The essential nature of each of these services, the risk of significant consumer detriment, and in some cases the limited nature of competition all mean that there will be a need for some form of consumer representation in these markets in the foreseeable future.

2.6 Table 1 maps out four market characteristics that together support the requirement for specialist consumer representation:
- the degree of monopoly power exercised within the market. Competition does not necessarily remove the need for consumer representation, but consumer bodies may be particularly important in monopoly sectors where customers cannot change suppliers;
- the extent to which the product is an essential service and the proportion of regulated activity that can be considered as such;

- informational problems and other supply side market failures that impact upon consumers e.g. mis-selling; and
- the size of the market.

Table 1: Market characteristics that justify sector-specific consumer representation

	Water	Energy	Post	Comms	Financial Services	Air
Degree of monopoly power	High	Medium	High	Low	Medium	Medium
Degree to which it is an essential service	High	High	Low	Low	Medium	Medium
Degree of information problems in the market	Medium	Low	Medium	Low	High	Medium
Market size (Annual household spend £m[9])	£5,493	£15,038	£884	£14,629	n/a	£10,590

- High
- Medium
- Low

2.7 This model, while simple, is helpful in understanding the need for different models of consumer representation in different markets. The degree to which each of these characteristics is present at a given point in time can help in assessing the necessary resources that should be channelled into consumer representation in a particular market.

Box 1: Applying the model to water and air travel

Limited competition in the water industry, together with the extent to which it is an essential service, supports the case for a relatively high level of consumer representation as compared to air transport, where these factors are less present. This does not suggest that consumer representation in air transport is unimportant, but that fewer resources may be needed to support it.

2.8 However, the model is not intended to encompass all relevant factors. There are a number of other factors that are relevant to decisions over consumer representation, such as:

- the degree of market maturity;
- the complexity of products and market institutions;
- the degree of infrastructure constraints that limit the exercise of competitive freedom; and
- the degree to which today's market developments may have longer-term implications.

2.9 It is important also to note that the market characteristics outlined in Table 1 are not set in stone. Indeed, effective consumer representation should seek to reduce consumer detriment and to press for increased competition, so that over the longer term the extent of sector specific consumer representation – and indeed regulation – may itself reduce. Market changes mean that new problems can arise, and competition will not necessarily eradicate all of the causes of consumer detriment. Nevertheless, the form of consumer representation in a sector – and the resources devoted to it – should be reviewed regularly over time to ensure it continues to be proportionate to need. An assessment of the risk of consumer vulnerability is also a valid consideration here.

3. Emerging issues

3.1 Since 1998, the sector-specific consumer bodies have registered significant achievements. The new bodies have established themselves, developing their own forward work programmes, increasing their credibility and recognition among stakeholders and establishing patterns of working. energywatch and Postwatch, in particular, have got to grips with the high levels of customer complaints that they received following establishment and receive generally positive feedback from customers about the service received[9].

3.2 Each of the consumer bodies is able to point to the positive effects that they have had on particular aspects of market behaviour or regulatory decisions. Examples of good practice are set out throughout this report. These achievements are testimony to the hard work and commitment of all those who work for these organisations.

---

9 Registering 84% and 79% customer satisfaction levels for energywatch and Postwatch respectively for their complaint and enquiry handling service. Source: PricewaterhouseCoopers benchmarking study, page 66.

> **Box 2: energywatch and doorstep selling**
>
> The decision to launch the **Stop Now!** campaign to stamp out poor selling practices was driven by a 50 per cent rise in complaints received by energywatch about marketing from January 2001 to October 2001. Towards the end of 2001 marketing and subsequent erroneous transfers were accounting for 40% of all energywatch complaints. energywatch launched the Stop Now! campaign in November 2001, with the aim of working in collaboration with the regulator, industry, MPs and other consumer groups to find workable solutions. The campaign was successful.
>
> As complaints relating to marketing continued to increase, energywatch called a summit in summer 2002 to assemble Chief Executives, Ofgem, the DTI and consumer groups to look for immediate solutions and impress on industry the seriousness of the issue. The Energy Minister, Brian Wilson, attended and issued the industry with an ultimatum to tackle mis-selling or face stiffer regulation. The outcome of this was an agreement between all parties to establish a Working Group to develop a code of practice, a training and registration programme for sales agents and a proposal to consider introducing compensation. Concurrently Ofgem was investigating London Electricity for breaches of the new marketing licence condition. energywatch provided Ofgem's investigation team with case studies and statistical analysis, resulting in Ofgem imposing a financial penalty on London Electricity of £2million for licence breaches. This was the first time that Ofgem had imposed a penalty since it gained full financial penalty powers earlier in the year.
>
> Since the summer of 2003 energywatch has worked closely with Ofgem in the development of a new marketing licence condition. Presentation and analysis of complaint statistics helped inform Ofgem's consultation document and subsequent decision document.

3.3 A number of issues have become apparent, however, in the operation of consumer representation in practice. These issues relate to the framework for consumer representation as a whole and the identification of such issues does not imply criticism of any individual consumer body or third party. Some of these issues are common to both consumer bodies and panels across regulated markets.

- The resources devoted to sectoral consumer representation are spread across five organisations and twenty seven regional offices[10]. This risks **dissipation of effort and duplication of resources**. Given that many of these organisations are small to start with, further fragmentation regionally risks a loss of economies of scale, increased costs and makes it difficult to develop strong institutional competences in areas such as project and programme management.
- Consumer representative bodies may become **unduly reactive**: responding either to the regulators' programme of consultation documents, or to complaints. An important source of added value from consumer representation is to highlight and bring to prominence those issues that could affect consumers in future, or that are not currently high on the regulators' list of priorities.
- Consumer bodies may target and attempt to influence those aspects of company performance or regulatory decision-making that are easiest to measure, rather than those which have the greatest positive impact on customers. Measuring performance, particularly in terms of delivering improved market outcomes has proved challenging in all sectors. Some consumer bodies do not currently have the processes in place to **measure impact** of their activities and campaigns.

3.4 Some issues appear to be more pertinent in those sectors where there are independent statutory bodies.

- Under the current statutory arrangements, some independent consumer bodies have a statutory duty to handle consumer complaints. In this circumstance, there is a risk that consumer representatives may spend too much of their time dealing with effects of consumer dissatisfaction (e.g. **complaints**). This may undermine incentives on suppliers to resolve customer concerns promptly and efficiently, if customers complain to the consumer body rather than to them, especially if the supplier perceives that the risk of regulatory intervention is low.
- A **confrontational relationship** can develop between the regulator and the consumer body. Although there will inevitably be disagreement on particular issues, the relationship is expected to be constructive. However, at times, difficult relations between consumer body and regulator have resul-

---

10 Some of the bodies do have a statutory obligation under current legislative arrangements to have one regional office in each of England, Wales, Scotland and Northern Ireland.

ted in reduced effectiveness of both[11]. An excessively adversarial stance can give rise to increased costs and delays and to the risk of undermining the credibility of the regulator.

3.5 Given the successes to date and also the emerging risks, this is an opportunity to step back and look strategically at how best to maximise the effectiveness of consumer representation across a range of regulated markets. For energywatch and Postwatch, the focus over the past three years has been on setting up the respective organisations and overcoming operational challenges. With these issues largely resolved, both bodies now recognise that the next stage of their development will involve adopting a more strategic approach in addressing systemic problems. This will build on achievements to date in terms of influencing the regulatory agenda and company behaviour. Equally, this is an opportunity for consumer bodies in air transport and financial services to build on the success of their organisations/panels and to ensure that they deliver real benefits to consumers and effect change in their respective markets. The new bodies currently being set up in communications and water can use the outcomes of this project to ensure that their organisations grow to be effective consumer advocates.

4. A vision for the future

4.1 The findings and recommendations of this report are focused on the effectiveness of consumer bodies over the next three to five years. These recommendations are underpinned by a vision of successful consumer representation that achieves measured improvements in the quality of services. This vision is of strategic and proactive consumer bodies, offering good value for money for the customer and operating within a framework that works well for all consumers.

4.2 Each of the organisations under consideration needs to become more strategic and proactive in its approach to consumer representation. This requires consumer bodies to concentrate resources where they are likely to have the biggest impact both for consumers generally and vulnerable consumers in particular. Consumer bodies need to monitor their outcomes and impact.

---

11 PricewaterhouseCoopers found evidence that the confrontational stance adopted towards each other by Postwatch, Postcomm and Royal Mail, in particular, has been a costly influencing strategy in terms of both time and money. Source: PwC benchmarking study, page 48.

4.3 It is essential that consumer bodies covered within the scope of this report demonstrate good value for money, particularly as customers or taxpayers ultimately provide their funding. In some sectors it will be necessary to look critically at the structure of regional representation. Where regional representation is required, consumer bodies need to maximise the benefits and ensure that such representation is cost effective and adds value to customers. Complaints handling must meet the needs of consumers for redress and advice, but must place clear incentives on companies to reduce consumer detriment and reduce the number of complaints being passed on to consumer bodies by delivering a high-quality service.

4.4 Lastly, the framework for consumer representation in regulated markets must work well for all consumers. Consumer bodies, regulators, companies and government need to work together in ensuring consumers are getting a good deal in regulated markets. Consumer bodies need to continue to engage strategically with regulators, companies, and other stakeholders in addressing market failures and consumer dissatisfaction at source. They also have an important role to play in empowering consumers.

4.5 The following sections set out how this vision may be delivered and focus on achieving greater effectiveness for the consumer bodies in the medium term. The recommendations in this report are based on best practice. They are not targeted at specific consumer bodies, and in some instances will have limited applicability to some bodies because of certain statutory duties or organisational arrangements in a particular sector.

5. Proactive and strategic consumer bodies

5.1 Consumer bodies have a wide remit and carry out a range of different functions, including policy influencing and campaigning; complaint-handling[12]; consumer education and research. To represent consumers effectively, they need to respond to customer needs and concerns; changes to the range, price and quality of products and services on offer; changes to Government policy and regulatory decisions and changes in the marketplace such as the level of competition.

5.2 However, with such a wide remit and a degree of overlap between consumer bodies and regulators that have a duty to promote consumers interests, it is

---

12 Postwatch, RPC, AUC, energywatch, WaterVoice only.

vital that consumer bodies ensure that they add value. Consumer bodies need to make clear, well-founded strategic choices about what they do and adopt a proactive approach to consumer advocacy, rather than solely reacting to external events. Complaint handling and research are important functions. However, they should provide the evidence base by which to support regulators in identifying and address underlying market failures, to increase consumer empowerment and to deliver change to the benefit of customers.

5.3 Figure 2 below illustrates the current allocation of resources by energywatch and Postwatch between their different functions. For energywatch the key drivers of costs are complaint-handling and overheads[13]. For Postwatch[14], complaint-handling and its work on the Post Office network are the largest activity drivers.

Figure 2: Allocation of expenditure between *energywatch* and *Postwatch* activities

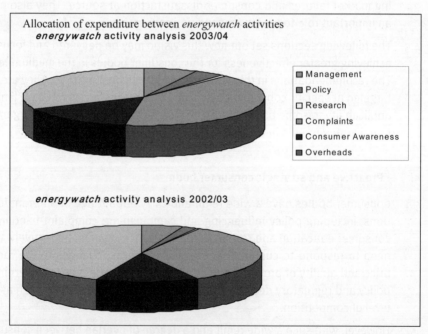

13 Source: PricewaterhouseCoopers Benchmarking study, figure 17. 40% of costs in 2003/04 allocated to complaints handling and 32% to Overheads.
14 Source: PricewaterhouseCoopers Benchmarking study, Figure 22. 15% of costs in 2003/04 allocated to Network and 19% to complaints handling.

A report by the Department of Trade and Industry and HM Treasury

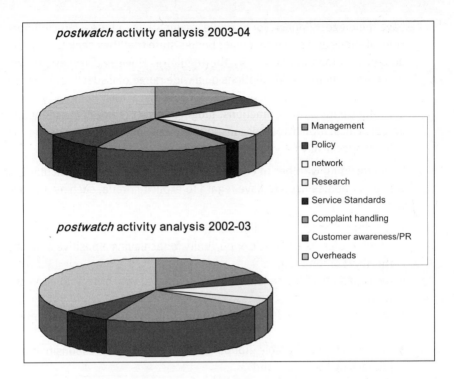

5.4 Over this period the main changes of expenditure for energywatch have been an increase in complaints handling costs from 35% of total spend in 2002/03 to 40% in 2003/04 and a decrease in overheads from 44% to 32%. For Postwatch, complaints handling costs have fallen from 23% to 19% over the same period.

Maximising impact

5.5 Consumer bodies are constantly faced with choices between competing demands on resources. Without clear prioritisation and leadership, consumer organisations may become involved in debates or issues than are not directly related to their core strategic objectives or that are best handled by another organisation. An expectation can develop that small bodies operating in the public arena – dealing with relatively complex markets that are often in the media spotlight – have to react to all market developments. It is sometimes difficult for such organisations to turn down these requests.

5.6 To ensure that consumer bodies effect real change for consumers in their respective markets they should concentrate their resources where they will have the biggest impact. For example, regulators generate a large number of consultations and some consumer bodies state that they seek to respond to all consultations generated by the regulator. However, in markets where there are numerous consultations on a wide range of issues[15], attempting to respond to all consultation documents could divert resources away from the consumer body's other functions. Judging impact is not necessarily an aggregate calculation across all consumer groups. Impact also needs to be considered specifically for vulnerable consumers.

5.7 When deciding whether to commit resources to address a particular issue, consumer bodies need to have regard to explicit criteria, such as the following:

- the degree of consumer detriment;
- whether there is a realistic opportunity for achieving a positive outcome in the short or long run;
- the capability of the consumer body, compared with others, to address the issue;
- degree to which the issue will be more suitably addressed by another organisation;
- the impact on vulnerable groups – and other statutory responsibilities – of addressing the issue; and
- the extent to which it is an issue of direct concern to consumers or is likely to be so in future.

These simple criteria could be developed by individual consumer bodies to devise a framework to assist in prioritising objectives and allocating resources. The OFCOM Consumer Panel have proposed a framework, based upon similar principles, by which they will prioritise their resources. This is illustrated in Box 3 below.

5.8 Campaigns and other proactive workstreams need to be founded on a strong evidence base. Good research is essential for the credibility of campaigns and for maximising impact. Complaints data can provide some valuable evidence for problems in regulated markets. However, complaints by their nature are self-selecting and backward-looking and should not be the sole or principal source of evidence. Complaints data alone may not be sufficient to identify all the issues that affect consumers adversely. In setting priorities, broadly based and forward-looking research is essential to complement the evidence of consumer detriment contained in complaints data.

---

15 For example, in April 2004 Ofgem had 19 'live' consultations; OFCOM had 14.

> **Box 3: Ofcom Consumer Panel**
>
> The Ofcom Consumer Panel, established under Communications Act 2003 has drawn up a short list of principles that will direct how it sets its priorities amongst the long list of things that it could tackle. Its proposed principles are:
>
> - **Relevance**: is this an issue that consumers have identified as a relevant concern in the annual Consumer Survey or which for other reasons the Panel believes is important for consumers?
> - **Detriment**: is there evidence of a real and significant risk of consumer detriment?
> - **Practicality**: is this a matter to which the Panel could add value (i.e. others are not already engaged on the consumer issue) and for which some practical solution can be found?
> - **Vulnerable groups**: would tackling an issue address the requirements and needs of consumers in one of the special categories they have identified?
>
> The Panel plans to inform itself about the current state of concern, and of knowledge, on the part of consumers in the communications marketplace. The Panel does not consider that complaints alone provide a sufficiently robust basis to underpin their policy development. The Ofcom Consumer Panel has decided that it will operate on the basis of research-based evidence.
>
> In order to do this, it will commission and manage a major piece of research across the whole market place. It is intended that this research will be repeated, probably on an annual basis, in order to give a developing picture of the marketplace from a consumers point of view.

5.9 A further initiative to bolster the evidence base and to increase transparency is to hold consumer committee meetings in public, as is the case with WaterVoice, for example. These open meetings allow consumers to hear at first hand the issues which the committees are proposing to address and – in WaterVoice meetings – to hear the views of the service providers.

5.10 Equally, it is essential that individual projects and campaigns are properly managed to ensure that results are delivered. PwC highlighted this as an area for improvement. Applying project management skills to individual objectives and campaigns ensures that resources and expertise are channelled properly and effectively. Project management includes the following steps:

- identifying, in a formal and consistent way, the desired outcomes at the start of any campaign;

- developing a detailed plan for achieving these outcomes;
- determining a methodology to test whether outcomes have been achieved satisfactorily;
- monitoring performance towards achieving the desired outcomes;
- evaluating the impact of each project, after completion.

5.11 To maximise benefits to consumers, it is necessary for sectoral consumer bodies to think creatively about the most effective means of achieving positive outcomes. For example, a consumer body may identify issues where the likelihood of achieving a positive outcome is constrained by barriers over which other stakeholders have more direct control. It may be most effective, in these circumstances, for the consumer body to bring these potential barriers – and their impact on customers – to the attention of these other stakeholders, before concentrating their own resources. In other cases, it may be possible to work in close partnership with another organisation that has closely aligned objectives, such as another consumer organisation or, in some instances, the regulator.

Recommendation 1

Consumer bodies should target resources where they will have the maximum impact, by:

- developing and publishing clear criteria by which they will prioritise activities;
- conducting rigorous research into those issues that currently have the greatest impact on consumer welfare and are likely to do so in the future and using this in formulating strategies and priorities;
- developing clear and complete forward work programmes in consultation with their main stakeholders;
- applying rigorous project and programme management techniques to all campaigns and activities and developing excellence in this area, possibly through joint training; and
- focusing on the outcomes for consumers of their actions, and the most effective means of securing those outcomes.

Measuring outcomes

5.12 Performance measurement is an important method by which consumer bodies can monitor the progress of their organisation and the success of particular initiatives. This is a challenging area for all sectoral consumer bodies. It is often more straightforward to measure inputs, or processes, rather than those outcomes that are often most important. Unlike private sector companies, there are no simple metrics, such as profitability or shareholder value, by which different types of activity can be compared. In achieving policy change, it can be difficult to disentangle the impact of any one organisation on the final outcome.

5.13 However, the existence of these challenges associated with measuring outcomes should not prevent consumer bodies and where appropriate their Departmental spending teams, from seeking to develop meaningful measures of performance, without which it is not possible to evaluate performance. To address the complexities associated with this issue, consumer bodies need at least three levels of performance indicators:

- To ensure operational effectiveness, consumer bodies should ensure they monitor performance of **operations**, for example consumer satisfaction with complaints handling. These indicators should be monitored over the longer term – and should remain consistent in terms of measurement.
- Outcome-focused performance indicators should be set for specific **campaigns or initiatives**. At the outset of each initiative, desired outcomes should be defined and indicators should be identified by which it would be possible to evaluate whether or not outcomes have been achieved. For example, when initiating a particular campaign, consumer bodies need to ask themselves what 'success would look like' and how they intend to measure progress toward meeting their desired outcomes.
- Consumer bodies also need to measure impact at an aggregate level. To be effective, consumer bodies need to be heard and respected by their key stakeholders. **Stakeholder surveys** provide a useful benchmark and feedback loop from those organisations that consumer bodies are seeking to influence.

> **Box 4: National Consumer Council's approach to measuring impact**
>
> PricewaterhouseCoopers identified the National Consumer Council's (NCC) approach to measuring impact as best practice. NCC measures *Impact* (on decision makers, on legislation, and on consumers) and their *Reputation* (as they consider that their reputation is directly related to the level of influence they are able to exert). To that end they have developed a hierarchy of performance measures and indicators for "Impact" and "Reputation", which aim to measure the outcomes of their work rather than focusing on outputs or processes.
>
> <u>Impact</u> is measured on a case study basis. Individual project quality, impact, and degree of influence exerted, are assessed through a variety of sources, e.g. meetings with stakeholders, seeking formal and informal feedback from partners and stakeholders, press cuttings and media reports. This material is used to develop an internal assessment of the project, and subsequently an external adviser will review and assess the project, in accordance with the following criteria:
>
> - whether the project was carried out to plan and timetable;
> - what issues arose on the project, and why, and evaluate how these issues were addressed;
> - what peer reviewers thought of the quality of NCC's work;
> - what reviewers thought of NCC's collaborative skills;
> - how much profile was generated and whether its tone was negative/positive, supportive or not;
> - how successful the project has been in influencing and achieving change; and
> - how the outputs were received by stakeholders.
>
> NCC considers its <u>reputation</u> to be a critical success factor for its ability to work with, and influence opinion-formers and decision-makers in a range of policy sectors across the UK. It is measured through a series of qualitative and quantitative surveys on decision makers and partnering consumer organisations whose views are sought on a range of factors, e.g. effectiveness, profile, strengths and weaknesses, to derive an assessment of its reputation. These surveys are repeated on an annual basis.

> **Recommendation 2**
>
> Consumer bodies and their spending teams should work together to develop meaningful measures of performance. To address the complexities associated with this issue, consumer bodies need three levels of performance indicator:
>
> - measures of operational effectiveness, which should be monitored over the longer term and should remain consistent in terms of measurement;
> - outcome-focused indicators of success for specific campaigns or initiatives; and
> - aggregate measures of impact and reputation, such as stakeholder surveys.

Supercomplaints

5.14 Consumer bodies should seek to use existing consumer and competition law to achieve change. For example the AUC have been proactive in the past engaging with the Office of Fair Trading as a route through which to secure good outcomes for consumers. Postwatch has also been proactive in working though OFT by submitting two informal super-complaints.

> **Box 5: AUC proactive initiative on airlines' contracts with passengers**
>
> The AUC had repeatedly pressed the European Commission to study airline conditions of carriage. A report, published in July 1997, concluded that a number of the terms of these contracts were unfair to passengers.
>
> In the light of this report, International Air Transport Association (IATA) task force reviewed IATA's own Recommended Practice on General Conditions of Carriage (RP1724). The changes to RP1724 that were subsequently adopted by IATA did not meet all of AUC's concerns. The Commission nevertheless remained unwilling to consider bringing forward any proposals for legislation at least until all other avenues for bringing about improvements had been explored. In particular, it looked to Member States to apply the EC Directive on Unfair Terms in Consumer Contracts to airlines' contracts with passengers.
>
> In January 1999, the AUC submitted a formal complaint to the Office of Fair Trading (OFT) about RP1724. The ensuing discussions between the OFT and IATA resulted in a new, more customer-friendly, version, which was formally adopted by IATA in June 2000.

5.15 The Super-complaint provisions are new under the Enterprise Act. Under the new legislation the relevant competition authorities must provide a formal response as to its proposed action within 90 days of receipt of a super-complaint submitted by designated appointees. The provision is an important tool by which consumer bodies can achieve positive outcomes providing an important channel whereby market intelligence gained by the consumer body can be fed into the regulatory process. Consumer bodies in regulated markets can use super-complaints to address systemic problems identified in the market through their own research, interface with consumers, or in some cases complaint-handling. They are in a strong position to gather the necessary evidence of a problem. The merits of these provisions need to be recognised by both consumer bodies *and* regulators. Super-complaints provide benefits to both parties:

- the process encourages consumer bodies to gather high quality data and provide a well-evidenced case by the prospect of a fair hearing; and
- a super-complaint is an opportunity for regulators to use this market intelligence to investigate reported problems in the market that are having a detrimental effect on consumers.

5.16 Energywatch and WaterVoice have applied for super-complaint status. There is a strong case for Postwatch also applying for super-complaint status. Consumer panels in financial services and communications, and the Air Transport Users Council should seek to develop partnerships with appointed bodies through which they could channel any potential super-complaint if and when necessary.

5.17 Alternative Dispute Resolution bodies (ADRs) such as Otelo and the Financial Ombudsmen Service may not meet the necessary criteria for super-complaint status due to their neutral status. However, these organisations collate and analyse important data on consumer experiences in their respective markets. It is vital that the regulator and consumer bodies continue to be able to harness this market intelligence, so that systemic problems emerging in a market can be identified and tackled.

> **Recommendation 3**
>
> The super-complaint provisions of the Enterprise Act provide opportunities for consumer bodies and regulators. To maximise this opportunity:
>
> - Postwatch should apply for super-complaint status;
>
> - consumer panels in financial services and communications, and the Air Transport Users Council should seek to develop partnerships with appointed bodies through which they could channel any potential super-complaint if and when necessary; and
>
> - market intelligence collated by Alternative Dispute Bodies (ADRs) should continue to be made available to regulators and consumer bodies on a timely and comprehensive basis.

6. Value for Money

6.1 Customers or taxpayers ultimately provide the funding for sectoral consumer bodies. It is therefore essential that their services represent good value for money. Over the past 3 years, the costs of running some of the consumer bodies have increased notably. This has largely been driven by increases in the number of complaints that have been unresolved between the companies and consumers, and that in some cases statutory consumer bodies have a duty to act upon. As a result it is timely to assess whether the current framework for consumer representation in the sectors covered by this report delivers value for money.

6.2 This section of the report draws largely on a study by PwC commissioned jointly by the DTI and NAO[16]. The focus of the PwC report was mainly on energywatch and Postwatch, although other sectoral consumer bodies were used for comparative purposes. As Table 2 shows, there are considerable differences between the budgets of the different consumer bodies. In 2003, these varied from £400,000 (Air Transport Users Council) to £12.4m (energywatch).

---

16 Benchmarking review of energywatch and Postwatch, March 2004. Available on the NAO website later this year.

Table 2: Income and Expenditure 2002/03

	E'watch	P'watch	W'voice[17]	AUC	FSCP
Geographic coverage	Great Britain	UK	England & Wales	UK	UK
Income £m	12.4	7.8	3.2	0.4	0.6
Expenditure £m[18]	10.9	7.8	3.2	0.4	0.6
Cost per household per annum £'s[19]	0.52	0.32	0.15	0.02	0.03
Cost as a % of total industry turnover	0.1%	0.9%	0.1%	0%	n/a
Consumer body expenditure as a % of Regulator spend	35%	130%	28%	3.6%	0.28%

6.3 While it is difficult to compare the costs of different models of consumer representation, evidence suggests that independent statutory bodies are approximately ten times more expensive to run than organisations embedded in the regulator, such as the Financial Services Consumer Panel. **This difference in costs is driven by two related factors: the extent of regional activity and the degree to which complaint handling is a core function of the consumer body.** Both of these are factors are driven to some extent by statutory duties. For example, consumer bodies in energy, postal services, and water have statutory obligations to handle complaints. These bodies are also required to have a minimum number of regional offices[20]. However, significant resources are devoted to maintaining regional office networks. For example, Postwatch has 113[21] staff across 9 offices, and energywatch has 303 staff in 8 offices. Typical activities for regional offices include complaint handling, liaison with local interests, monitoring of local issues and providing support to regional committees[22].

---

17   The new Consumer Council for Water established in the Water Act 2003 is expected to cost in the region of £6m when it is up and running in 2005.
18   Excludes non-cash adjustments of depreciation.
19   Based upon 21.7m households in England and Wales and 2.2 in Scotland, Northern Ireland 0.6m (Census 2001).
20   Energywatch and Postwatch are required to have one office and one committee in England, Wales, Scotland (and Northern Ireland for post). WaterVoice is required to have regional offices in England and Wales only.
21   Figure excludes 15.5 casual posts (mostly for Network Reinvention support work.)
22   Energywatch does not have regional committees.

A report by the Department of Trade and Industry and HM Treasury

6.4 Sectoral consumer bodies add most value through their roles in developing policy and influencing stakeholders, in relation to systemic market failures. Their activities in handling enquiries and complaints from individual consumers are important in informing this work. Access to redress is also important for consumers. The organisational design of these bodies should, however, give primacy to the key value adding role of policy development and influencing.

6.5 The costs of complaint handling and of maintaining a regional network of offices account for a high proportion of the total expenditure of energywatch and Postwatch, as can be seen from Table 3 below. Cost of complaint handling in Financial Services and Telecomms is borne by alternative dispute resolution schemes such as the Financial Ombudsmen Service.

Table 3: Costs of handling complaints and maintaining a regional presence[23]

		energywatch[24] £m		Postwatch £m	
		2002-03	2003-04	2002-03	2003-04
Total costs for the year		10.9	13.0	8.2	10.2
Regional	Complaint handling	3.7	5.3	1.5	1.2
	Other	1.9	2.4	0.6	1.3
Total regional cost (% of total cost for the year)		5.6 (51%)	7.7 (59%)	2.1 (26%)	2.5 (24%)
Central office	Complaint handling	-	-	0.4	0.7
	Other	5.3	5.2	5.7	7.1
Total complaint handling (% of total cost for the year)		3.7 (34%)	5.3 (41%)	1.9 (23%)	1.9 (18%)

6.6 As Table 3 shows there are significant complaint-handling functions undertaken within regional offices. This may be less efficient than consolidating the function into one single location. In making an assessment of the purpose and value for money of regional structures, it is therefore important to consider first the complaint-handling functions. For those bodies with regional offices, the amount of pure regional activity relating to complaints handling is small.

---

23 Source: PricewaterhouseCoopers benchmarking report, page 4, figure 2 and 4.
24 Energywatch regional costs exclude accommodation costs, which were £1,058,000 in 2003/04.

Enquiries and Complaint-handling

6.7 Handling enquiries and complaints is the principal way in which sectoral consumer bodies have direct contact with consumers. Enquiries include information requests and giving advice. Complaints on the other hand involve a greater input from the sectoral consumer body through engaging with the relevant supplier on behalf of the consumer.

Table 4: Comparative enquiry and complaint-handling data in 2002/03

	No. of Enquiries	No. of Complaints
Energywatch	70,840	109,578
Postwatch	13,101	40,178
WaterVoice	32,944	9,679
AUC	5,332	

6.8 Complaint handling is a key aspect of the regulatory system that needs to work well. It is also the most visible test of the effectiveness of a consumer body:

- consumers need to have the skills to be able to identify and take up their complaints against suppliers;
- vulnerable consumers need support in identifying problems and formulating complaints;
- companies should deal with these complaints adequately; and
- disputes need to be resolved quickly and effectively.

From the consumer's perspective, it is important that the different facets of a complaint are dealt with smoothly and efficiently. Equally, it is important that the right incentives are in place to ensure that companies respond quickly to rectify consumer complaints and to stem complaints at source.

6.9 In the initial start-up phase for energywatch and Postwatch, there has been an understandable focus on making these organisations and their services known to consumers as far as possible. The level of complaints received by both Postwatch (from 9,944[25] in 2001/02[26] to 61,000 in 2003/04), and energywatch (from 74,749 in 2000/01 to 90,000 in 2003/04) can be taken, in part, as evidence of increasing consumer awareness of the consumer bodies

---

25 12,420 in 15 months to 31/3/2002.
26 Figure relates to a fifteen month period to 31 March 2002.

and of the help which they can give with unresolved complaints. A natural consequence of the increased numbers of complaints has been the devotion of considerable resources to complaint handling.

6.10 As these sectoral consumer bodies have begun to move on from the start-up phase, their focus has shifted away from being complaint-handling organisations, towards addressing consumer issues and concerns at source. Clearly, there needs to be a recognition that dealing with unresolved complaints on the current scale does not reflect success for the regulatory system overall. It is necessary for all stakeholders to develop a strategy to achieve a step change in complaint handling.

6.11 It is essential that companies in regulated markets should be incentivised to deal with their own complaints quickly and effectively. Unless there are complaint-handling procedures operated by the companies that are comparable with the best in the private sector, these companies will not provide the standard of service that consumers require and deserve. It will always be more difficult and time consuming for a consumer body to press home a legitimate complaint compared with a company dealing with it in-house. Companies must accept complete responsibility for resolving differences with their customers, and take the opportunity of the personal contact afforded by the dialogue to receive feedback and enhance the reputation of the company. In the water sector for instance, there is a statutory requirements for all water companies to have complaint handling procedures approved by Ofwat, after consultation with WaterVoice. This requirement is a key part of the strategy for getting water companies to resolve customer complaints effectively.

6.12 However, there will continue to be role for third parties in handling complaints and consumer enquiries. Inevitably, there will be a residual number of complaints that require resolution between consumers and companies. Vulnerable consumers need to be supported in taking forward complaints. At present, consumer bodies in air, energy, post and water carry out these functions. However, there is an opportunity for more efficient delivery of this role.

6.13 At present, the consumer bodies handle in total approximately 115,000 enquires per year at an average cost per enquiry of £57[27]. From 2006-07, Consumer Direct will provide a common, one-stop first port of call for all con-

---

27 Source: PWC Benchmarking study, figure 26.

sumer enquiries. This should enable the necessary re-alignment of resources within consumer bodies. It is envisaged that Consumer Direct will provide an accessible and cost-effective way of handling first tier enquiries and advice on behalf of individual consumer bodies, although, in practice, this will have to be tested.

6.14 There is also an opportunity to ensure that the delivery of complaint-handling function is as efficient and effective as possible. Handling complaints regionally prevents the exploitation of economies of scale and requires strong central management and control, not only to manage the varying workloads, but also to ensure that there is effective communication of best practice and latest developments across the organisation. These costs of handling complaints at a regional level appear to outweigh any associated benefits: for example, Postwatch estimates that 80 per cent of complaints received are of a general nature, rather than region-specific[28].

Alternative Dispute Resolution mechanisms

6.15 In other markets, notably financial services and telecoms, consumers are represented by consumer panels, which are incorporated within the sectoral regulators. In these sectors, Alternative Dispute Resolution bodies (ADRs) handle complaints. The core role for an ADR (an ombudsman in the case of telecoms and financial services) is to investigate and resolve, determine or make recommendations with regard to those complaints that the Ombudsman is empowered to investigate.

6.16 This approach to dealing effectively with disputes between customers and utility suppliers is also used in other countries. In Australia, for example, the Energy and Water Ombudsman (Victoria) facilitates resolution of complaints between consumers of electricity, gas, and water in the state of Victoria and those service providers who are members of the scheme. As with the UK Telecomms and Financial Services sectors, it is a condition of the relevant electricity and gas licences that the companies must be members of an appropriate ombudsman scheme. The costs of the scheme are borne by member companies and authorities according to the number of complaints raised against each member.

---

28 Source: PwC benchmarking study, page 22.

> **Box 6: Complaints handling in the telecommunications and financial services sector**
>
> Under EC Directive 2002/22/EC and sections 52 and 53 of the Communications Act all telecommunications companies that have domestic or small business customers, will be required to be a member of a dispute resolution body.
>
> The first such ADR, Otelo, is run and funded by major telecoms companies, and is approved by Ofcom and underpinned by legislation in the Communications Act 2003. Otelo determines complaints cases – their findings are binding on companies but not consumers – which are referred by consumers or service providers where there is failure to reach agreement on resolution of a complaint. Because Otelo is partly funded by subscription from the companies (currently set to recover 20% of budgeted costs) and partly by a charge on the relevant service provider (set to recover the remaining 80%) for each complaints case referred for action, there is a very strong incentive for service providers to resolve complaints from customers efficiently and to the customer's satisfaction. Otelo is the first established ombudsman for telecoms, but other, similar, schemes may be set up by the industry subject to the approval of the regulator. The Otelo model provides a practical example of what can be achieved by an industry-funded ADR.
>
> In financial services, the Financial Ombudsman Service operates a similar scheme. Like Otelo, It is funded partly by subscription from member companies, and partly by a charge on the relevant service provider for each complaints case referred for action.
>
> Generally, Ombudsman decisions on individual complaints are binding on the service provider and the consumer, only if the consumer accepts them. Consumers retain the option to reject the Ombudsman-recommended solution and adopt a different resolution route, perhaps through action in the courts. Sectoral consumer bodies do not have the same powers to determine outcomes for consumers, in part because they do not have the same degree of neutrality as an ADR body.

6.17 Companies should be at the forefront of handling complaints effectively. Only more complex cases should need to be referred to the consumer bodies or an ADR body, as appropriate. Consumer bodies should focus on improving the performance of companies in complaint handling, and should consider how best to handle dispute resolution.

> **Recommendation 4**
>
> Consumer representative bodies should work together with support of regulators and sponsor departments to develop a new strategy for complaint-handling, based on the following principles:
>
> - companies in each sector should bear primary responsibility for handling complaints efficiently and effectively. There should be strong incentives on companies to adopt best practice in complaint-handling;
> - Consumer Direct will become the one-stop shop for all first tier consumer enquiries. Consumer Direct could deal with the majority of such enquiries with reduced need for referral to specialist bodies; and
> - complaints-handling by consumer bodies should be further consolidated regionally within each body to exploit economies of scale.

Regional structure

6.18 Postwatch, energywatch and WaterVoice each operates a network of regional offices across England and Wales and, as appropriate, Scotland and Northern Ireland. These regional offices often handle complaints from consumers in their particular catchment area, liase with local stakeholders, engage with consumers and in some cases provide secretariat support to regional committees. Postwatch and WaterVoice each operate regional committees, which they use to support complaint investigation, to monitor performance of suppliers in their areas, to engage with local stakeholders and to identify issues of local concern to consumers, referring to their National Council for consideration where appropriate.

6.19 **Table 5** below shows the location of regional offices for the four largest consumer bodies. There is some degree of common location in some of the cities chosen but there is also a degree of diversity.

Table 5: Regional offices

Regional office locations	energywatch (8 offices) GB	Postwatch (9 offices) UK	WaterVoice (9 offices) England & Wales
London	**	**	*
Glasgow	*		
Edinburgh		*	
Cardiff	*	*	*
Belfast		*	
Newcastle	*		
Darlington			*
York			
Bradford		*	
Manchester	*		*
Birmingham	*		**
Stafford		*	
Bristol			*
Bournemouth	*		
Weymouth		*	
Exeter			*
Cambridge			*
Ely		*	

Key: * denotes one office; ** denotes two

Note: energywatch has a statutory obligation to maintain at least one office in each of England, Scotland and Wales (Utilities Act 2000, s.18(4)). Postwatch is required to maintain at least one office in each of England, Scotland, Wales, and Northern Ireland (Postal Services Act 2000 s.54(6)).

6.20 A regional presence may be appropriate and necessary, depending on the nature of the market failures being addressed. The Government believes that policy design should take place at the level at which the market failure is most effectively tackled. This principle was set out in March 2004 in "Devolving Decision-making: 2 – Meeting the regional economic challenge: Increasing regional and local flexibility". This principle can be applied to the delivery of sectoral consumer representation. The need for a regional network of offices to deliver operations will depend on the level at which the market failure is occurring; the locus of decision making within a particular market and whether it is efficient to do so. For example, providing it is cost efficient to do so, there may be a justification for regional representation in the water sectors given that the sector is compromised of regional monopolies.

Consumer Representation in Regulated Industries

6.21 There are a number of potential benefits from such regional structures[29]:

- local capacity is available to deliver consumer awareness and education programmes;
- regional communications functions are effective in maintaining relationships with the regional media;
- links with Scottish Executive and Welsh Assembly;
- regional resources enable consumer bodies to maintain close links with suppliers where suppliers are regionally based; and
- regional committees in water and postal services can undertake important work in relation to specific local issues – for example the urban and rural network closure programme.

6.22 However, a regional structure also gives rise to some costs that would not otherwise arise. Within a total operating budget of £13m, the direct costs of energywatch's regional offices are £7.7m. Within Postwatch's overall budget of £10.3m, the direct costs of its regional offices are £2.5m[30]. There are also indirect costs associated with regional operations in terms of head office staff resource required to support them[31]. Therefore benefits and costs of regional delivery need to be examined carefully on an issue-by-issue basis.

6.23 There is some evidence that regional representation, for example through regional committees, can have benefits for the effectiveness of some sectoral consumer bodies. Regional committee members are likely to be able to bring to bear a breadth and depth of knowledge to local issues that is valuable to the development of policy at the national level. There is also evidence that regional input has been important in gathering information and in linking with local media, for example in Postwatch's *Urban Reinvention* programme.

6.24 A continued regional presence can therefore add value, in particular when the consumer experience has a regional dimension. Regional committee members are often well placed to provide local expertise and key media and partnership contacts. This is an important aspect of regional representation: the maintenance of strong links with devolved administrations and local opinion formers, as well as reflecting distinctly regional issues and nuances in the contribution to national strategy and policy development.

---

29 Source: PwC Benchmarking Report, page 96.
30 Excluding its call centre in Northern Ireland and its outsourced offices.
31 For example in providing back-office services such as finance, HR etc. and in ensuring best practice in relation to complaint handling.

> **Box 7: Postwatch work on Urban Reinvention – adding value at a regional level**
>
> Approximately 15 per cent of Postwatch's budget is allocated to the Network Directorate, which consists of 15 staff members, 13 of whom are deployed on the Urban Reinvention Programme. They monitor and respond to developments in the UK's network of 17,500 Post Offices.
>
> While the Government provides a limited subsidy to the rural network in order to fulfil its commitment to 'no avoidable closures', it continues to work towards achieving its strategy for long term sustainable future growth. A key component of this strategy is its 'urban reinvention' which is undertaken in urban areas with an uneven spread of post offices: while some areas are marked by a disproportionate number of post offices to population, others have an insufficient number. The programme aims to correct this imbalance, with a reduction from 9,000 to 6,000 Post Offices by the end of 2004.
>
> There is evidence that Postwatch's engagement in this programme has had significant beneficial impact, for example in identifying and addressing problems of implementation i.e. in accordance with the original programme objectives, and in successfully opposing some closures and asking for modifications. As a result of the large number of complaints from MPs and consumers alike, Post Office Ltd. committed to immediately implement a revised urban reinvention procedure containing some key improvements.

6.25 There is little evidence, on the contrary, to support the delivery of complaint-handling at a regional level. Most consumers simply want an effective and efficient complaints-handling and dispute resolution service. Given that a high proportion of complaints, particularly in energy and post, are of a national nature, there could be benefits in consolidating of complaint-handling functions in one location. This would promote flexible use of resources in this resource-intensive function, as well as facilitating efficient and consistent treatment of similar types of complaints.

6.26 A network of small regional offices also presents challenges with regard to consistency of operations between offices; a high cost base due to lack of economies of scale; and also problems for co-ordination. Removal of the complaints-handling function would have resource implications for those offices. Where there is a demonstrable need to maintain some regional office presence, the question further arises of whether each individual organisation alone can efficiently provide a critical mass of staff to maintain an effective presence. Consolidation of regional offices into fewer but larger offices may bring benefits. For example, the support functions for regional committees do not need to be provided by dedicated regional offices. This can be seen from the experience of WaterVoice, which supports two regional committees from one office in Darlington[32]. The Government has recently announced the future structure and organisation of the new Consumer Council for Water established in the Water Act 2003. The new structure includes a consolidation of the number of existing offices and committees of WaterVoice[33].

6.27 Alternatively, it may be desirable for those consumer bodies with an evident need for regional offices to co-locate or secure common functions in order to maximise synergies and economies of scale and scope.

6.28 There may also be opportunities for realising some of the benefits of a regional structure through alternative channels. For example, the advent of Consumer Direct will provide an important new service to consumers who seek advice, simplifying the "front end" of specialist services and providing a consistent service in all parts of England, Scotland, and Wales.

Recommendation 5

Consumer bodies must ensure that regional representation continues to offer good value for money for consumers:

- markets that do not have a clear regional structure do not require a regional network of offices for consumer representation;
- regional operations should focus on those market failures and aspects of the consumer experience that differ substantially between regions;
- complaints handling should be conducted centrally and not dispersed amongst regional offices;
- where regional committees are required, the consumer bodies should consider whether these committees require secretariat support from separate regional offices. Options for efficiency gains include:
    - consolidation of the number of offices with regional offices supporting more than one committee; and
    - consumer bodies pooling resources to provide secretariat support to regional committees.

---

32 Source: PwC report on the new Consumer Council for Water.
33 Source: http://www.defra.gov.uk/news/2004/040407c.htm.

7. A regulatory framework that works well for all consumers

7.1 Consumer bodies operate alongside a diverse set of stakeholders, including customers, companies, regulators and Government. Although the interests of these stakeholders do not coincide on all issues, they all share a common objective: to ensure that consumers are getting a good deal. It is arguably only by achieving greater understanding and co-operation between these stakeholders that a step change in consumer satisfaction can be achieved.

7.2 It is therefore vital that consumer bodies engage strategically with all of those stakeholders that have the powers to effect change. There are three aspects to this:
- empowered consumers;
- strategic partnerships with Government and regulators; and
- constructive but challenging relationship with suppliers.

Empowered Consumers

7.3 Consumers need the skills, knowledge and information to be able to make effective choices in the market and stand up for their rights. This is better for both consumers and for companies. It is important that consumer bodies work together to achieve this goal, as there are significant synergies from joint working in this area.

7.4 The importance of consumer empowerment was recognised in the Consumer White Paper, which stated "well-informed consumers help markets to work effectively. Customers who can assert their needs clearly and make the best choices spur business to become more competitive and raise productivity. Consumers benefit from this through lower prices, increased choice and more innovative products."

7.5 The benefits from consumer empowerment apply just as much to regulated markets as to other sectors of the economy. Sectoral consumer bodies therefore need to focus on empowering consumers by:
- providing consumers with the information and advice that will enable them to operate confidently in regulated markets and to address problems directly with companies;
- supporting vulnerable consumers; and
- where possible, promoting competition and switching between suppliers.

There are significant synergies in terms of consumer empowerment from working with other consumer bodies. This is therefore an area where sectoral consumer bodies could jointly provide campaigns or other empowerment functions.

7.6 Consumers need **access to information** along with the necessary skills and knowledge of their rights, to enable them to identify and tackle problems and complaints directly. WaterVoice has recently published a leaflet, in January 2004, which sets out what water consumers should expect from water companies. This information allows consumers to ensure they understand what levels of service their water companies should be delivering and therefore when to challenge if a water company is not meeting necessary standards.

7.7 Consumer Direct has been established to provide a high quality national service to meet this need, across all sectors. A key objective for Consumer Direct is to meet unmet demand for information, and, by generating a high level of awareness, reach out to the 50% of all consumers who simply do not know where to look for advice and information.

> **Box 8: Consumer Direct**
>
> Consumer Direct is a new national telephone and on-line consumer information and advice service. Delivered in partnership with local authorities and other advice agencies, it will be the first point of call for consumers, delivering first tier advice on a range of consumer matters, including advice before shopping and information on consumer rights, and practical guidance on individual problems and how to solve them.
>
> Consumer Direct will:
>
> - increase consumers' access to quality assured advice and information;
> - aim to give people the knowledge, tools and confidence to be able to resolve matters themselves;
> - improve the quality and coverage of information for Trading Standards and other stakeholders ; and
> - act as a gateway to other complementary services where further help is required or specialist advice is needed.
>
> The service will begin operation in Scotland, Wales, Southwest England, and Yorkshire and the Humber in Summer 2004, with nationwide rollout completed by 2006-07.
>
> Consumer Direct will be a key driver of consumer empowerment by increasing access to advice and information. Consumer bodies should use Consumer Direct as one channel by which to deliver empowerment initiatives, for example, by ensuring that Consumer Direct advisors have access to sector specific leaflets and information

7.8 Sectoral consumer bodies need to ensure consumers have access to information on how to complain in their sectors, and the information that they will need to support a complaint. To achieve this, consumer bodies need both to ensure the right information is available, and to ensure the widest possible access to that information. Companies will often readily agree that direct feedback from consumers is an important source of information that enables them to identify and address problems early. Good customer service should be a source of comparative advantage and consumer bodies should therefore encourage and support customers to engage with companies directly.

7.9 Empowering consumers is one area where there are significant synergies to be achieved from joint working between sectoral consumer bodies. Sectoral consumer bodies should actively look to exploit the reach of other generalist organisations tasked with empowering consumers – such as Consumer Direct or OFT.

7.10 With the aim of promoting wider access, the OFT has set up an area of their website for the adviser community. The website will provide factual material prepared by OFT and other consumer organisations on the main consumer rights/advice issues. The material will be available for use or adaptation by other groups tailoring it to match their target audiences. The website will allow better communication between different providers of information and advice, leading in principle to the sharing of best practice and the reduction of wasteful duplication. Areas in which joint working might pay dividends include educating consumers about their rights and learning from experience of others in communicating with vulnerable groups.

7.11 **Increasing competition** in many of the utility sectors has provided significant benefits for many consumers. Consumers increasingly have a choice of suppliers, and an array of different tariffs from which to choose. Consumer bodies have an important role to play in providing the high quality information and advice needed if consumers are to take full advantage of competitive markets. Influential consumer councils and well-informed consumers can play a key part in competitive markets, in improving standards and lowering prices.

7.12 Consumer bodies should promote pro-active consumers and champion the benefits to consumers of switching suppliers. Consumer bodies can play an important role in providing consumers with the tools to enable them to make decisions on suppliers. For example, the energywatch website currently has a user-friendly web-based tool to enable consumers to find out the prices that different suppliers charge for different levels of energy usage in a particular area. Another example of good practice in this area is the Consumers Association, who currently operate a 'Switch with Which' campaign aimed at mobile phones, energy suppliers, mortgages and current accounts.

7.13 A particular challenge lies in **empowering vulnerable groups**. Vulnerable consumers may be less receptive to mainstream channels of advice and information provision. There may be lessons to be learnt for other sectors from the 'Reachout' programme, led by energywatch.

Recommendation 6

Consumer bodies should work closely with other stakeholders to increase consumer empowerment, through:

- campaigning with each other and with other organisations charged with empowering consumers, to raise consumer awareness of their rights and the benefits of being an active and demanding consumer. In particularly by contributing to and using the OFT website for consumer advisor and using Consumer Direct as a delivery channel for information and advice.
- making widely available – through their websites, Consumer Direct and otherwise – information for customers on how to switch suppliers and how to complain about poor service.
- developing partnerships with bodies such as Age Concern and Citizen's Advice Bureaux, to reach out to vulnerable groups, such as the elderly and ethnic minorities.

Strategic partnerships with regulators and Government

7.14 In energy and postal services, the consumer bodies are fully independent from the Regulator. This places consumer bodies in a strong position to be able to argue the case of the consumer with the regulator; raises the profile of consumers in regulatory decision-making and encourages more open debate on regulatory decision. However, to be fully effective, regulators, sponsoring government departments and consumer bodies need to work very closely together to achieve their common aims.

7.15 There will be occasions when these organisations have differences in perspective or objectives, and there will inevitably be instances of tension between these parties. In general, however, the interests of these three stakeholders should be broadly aligned and the relationship should be that of a mature and trusting strategic partnership.

7.16 A number of practical steps can be taken to strengthen and deepen these partnerships over and above the Memorandum of Understanding that already exist. A first step is to recognise the interdependence and shared interest of these three bodies. This can be achieved through, where appropriate, agreeing joint work programmes between consumer bodies, regulators and Government to address issues of shared concern. Regulators and consumer bodies may agree shared objectives and targets in relation to particular objectives – for example switching suppliers – in securing a better deal for consumers. Measures such as this would help ensure that stakeholders work together towards a joint goal.

7.17 A second step is to develop and demonstrate trust and mutual recognition. In some instances (such as water) the consumer body and the regulator have agreed a "no surprises" policy, where advance notice of announcements is given by each party to the other. This does not confer a right of veto, but facilitates informed debate on initiatives, and avoids the problems associated with diverting attention from the issue to an apparent disagreement between the regulator and the consumer body. An effective 'no surprises' policy between consumer bodies, regulators and Government is an essential factor in building trust.

7.18 Equally importantly is establishing the consumer bodies' 'right to be heard'. In Water, the Director General of Ofwat, attends the WaterVoice Council meetings to listen to views and answer questions. The minutes of these meetings are published. Alternatively, as part of the annual reporting process, consumer bodies could set out their comments and recommendations to the regulator based on policy issues arising during the forthcoming year. The regulator could then present a formal reply to these recommendations. This approach is followed by the FSA and FSA Consumer Panel.

Box 9: FSA Consumer Panel annual report – right to be heard

The Financial Services and Markets Act 2000 established that the regulator must consider representations made by the Consumer Panel and – if the regulator disagrees with a view expressed or proposal made in the representation, it must give the Panel a statement in writing of its reasons for disagreeing.

In practice, the Annual Report of the FSA Consumer Panel provides a commentary on the work of the FSA, and makes representations. The FSA then lists and responds to these representations in its own Annual Report, providing a valuable, transparent, means of formal dialogue to supplement the ongoing discussions between the bodies.

7.19 A third area for closer cooperation between regulators and consumer bodies is in Europe. While consumer bodies, regulators and Government may not always agree entirely on all aspects of a policy area, there will often be key areas of common ground. A joint approach to negotiating with EU partners might strengthen the position of each of the individual organisations and the overall impact of UK lobbying. Wherever possible consumer bodies should explore opportunities to engage with Government and regulators to developing joint negotiating positions on EU directives where appropriate.

Recommendation 7

Consumer bodies should deepen and strengthen their strategic partnerships with regulators and Government, through all or some of the following:

- agreeing joint work programmes, where appropriate, between consumer bodies, regulators and Government to address issues of shared concern;
- committing to shared objectives and targets in relation to particular objectives in securing a better deal for consumers;
- operating an effective 'no surprises' policy between consumer bodies, regulators and Government;
- inviting the Regulator and or other key stakeholders to council meetings and publishing the minutes of that meeting;
- setting out through the annual reporting process their comments and recommendations to the regulator, with the expectation of receiving a formal reply to these recommendations; and
- wherever possible developing joint negotiating positions with other consumer bodies, regulators or Government where appropriate on EU directives.

Constructive but challenging relationship with suppliers

7.20 Consumers' experience of markets is dominated by their engagement with companies. In a competitive market, company performance is largely driven by consumer demands. Those companies not serving the needs of their customers will lose out to alternative providers. In the absence of perfect competition, consumer bodies have an active role to play in engaging with companies, and in holding them to account. This can be particularly salient in the case where there is no or limited competition, for example water and postal services.

7.21 Working with companies gives consumer bodies the opportunity to improve the consumer experience at source. Consumer bodies and companies should recognise that the responsibility for serving the needs of consumers lies firmly with the provider. However, in the absence of effective competition in the supply of essential services, these incentives are not always present or recognised by companies. The regulator is responsible for ensuring that companies have the right incentives to ensure consumers are getting a good deal and experience high quality service. The consumer body can play an important role in putting these incentives in place.

7.22 There are many different ways in which consumer bodies can engage with companies to enhance consumer experience and ultimately company performance. First, consumer bodies could negotiate minimum service standards with companies governing their interface with consumers. This could be carried out in conjunction with the regulator. Service standards could then be monitored and reviewed by the respective consumer bodies as part of a 'consumer audit'. The WaterVoice practice of auditing the individual complaint handling systems in each water company, and publishing the results, provides a firm discipline on the companies in the sector and provides a means of benchmarking best practice.

> **Box 10: WaterVoice engaging with Suppliers**
>
> WaterVoice regional committees currently audit the complaint-handling function of companies. The results are used by Ofwat in assessing company performance.
>
> The WaterVoice committees visit the customer departments of the companies and look at what they are doing, inspect records and give views on whether they are handling complaints properly. That is something that the Regulator will then take into account as part of the qualitative assessment of how well the companies are performing their job in relation to their customers. WaterVoice also review companies debt management procedures and other areas of consumer service.
>
> In addition, WaterVoice regional committees hold annual meetings with the boards of the relevant water companies, including non-executives. This provides a direct means of informing non-executives in particular, about the issues of concern to consumers.

7.23 Second, publishing comparative information on company performance is a powerful accountability mechanism. Energywatch and the new Consumer Council for Water have a statutory duty to publish comparative data on company performance and complaints received. Energywatch also publish comparative price tables on their website.

7.24 Lastly, consumer bodies can also engage at board level with companies to address systemic problems with customer service and to discuss developments in the marketplace – such as technological or legal developments – and their impact on consumers.

> **Recommendation 8**
>
> Consumer bodies should engage strategically with companies to deliver better outcomes for consumers by:
>
> - where practicable, working with the relevant regulator and companies to agree a programme of audit of complaint and customer-service procedures in each company, with a view to spreading best practice;
> - publishing comparative information on company performance; and
> - engaging with companies at board level to address systemic problems with customer services and highlight upcoming issues.

Consumer Representation in the EU

7.25 It is widely recognised that the consumer voice across the European Community is relatively weak, particularly compared to the UK. There is a need to strengthen consumer representation in some other Member States and the Commission. Consumer bodies have an important responsibility to represent consumer interests at the EU level and to ensure that the European Commission is informed of them. However, this can be resource intensive for consumer representatives in the UK.

7.26 The European Consumer Consultative Group (ECCG) is the Commission's main forum for engaging with consumer organisations. Functions of the ECCG include providing the Commission with advice, guidance, and opinions on issues affecting consumers and to inform the Commission about developments in consumer policy in Member States.

7.27 Other consumer organisations having a presence at EU level include the Bureau Europeen des Unions des Consommateurs (BEUC) where the NCC and Consumers' Association are members, and the Association of European Consumers, where there is a UK member of the board from the Food Commission.

7.28 The Commission considers that consumer participation within Commission consultative bodies and working groups will help to ensure integration of consumer concerns in all EU policies. Consultative bodies have been set up in fields including transport, energy, and telecommunications.

7.29 There does seem to be considerable opportunity – and need – to present a coherent consumer view at the European level. In addition to the formal institutional arrangements, there is scope for making unofficial links and for lobbying. Building up personal links is critical to effective engagement in Europe, and there is scope for work at this level by both consumer bodies alone, and through joint initiatives with regulators and Government to secure successful outcomes for consumers.

> **Recommendation 9**
> - Consumer bodies should seek full engagement at the EU level, whether alone or through joint action with other consumer bodies, regulators and Government.

8. Longer-term issues

8.1 This project has taken an explicitly medium-term focus, building on the success of the existing sectoral consumer bodies and maximising the effectiveness of consumer representation going forward. Nonetheless, it is important that the consumer bodies look ahead to potential future market developments in determining their strategies and operations. The Government must also continue to assess whether the framework for consumer representation is responsive to consumer needs and continues to be efficient and effective. This section presents a long-term vision for the future of consumer representation, which is intended to form a starting point for discussion.

8.2 As this report has highlighted, consumer representation is fragmented, largely as a result of sector specific legislation. The scope of this study has enabled a thorough review of arrangements across sectors, thus benefiting from a cross-cutting perspective. As a result, the DTI/HM Treasury review has identified an alternative delivery mechanism for achieving the Governments objectives for consumer representation set out in the White Paper published as part of the Utilities Review. This scenario is based upon the synergies identified during the study between different representative bodies and also a consideration of the drivers of change over the medium to longer-term.

8.3 This longer-term scenario includes the establishment of a National Utilities Consumer Council (NUCC) to undertake consumer advocacy across a number of sectors. The NUCC would play a key role in consumer advocacy and scrutiny of Regulators, Government and companies. Under this model, Alternative Dispute Resolution (ADRs) bodies could provide an efficient and effective redress mechanism for consumers with unresolved complaints in regulated markets.

8.4 However, it is important to recognise that any introduction of ADRs points towards a consolidation of the number of existing consumer bodies. What must be avoided is an inefficient proliferation of institutions that could both increase the complexity for consumers and lead to the regulator being less informed about consumer issued than they should be.

Long-term scenario for consumer representation

8.5 There are a number of different drivers for change in the context of consumer representation in future years.

- First, there will be national roll-out of Consumer Direct by 2006-07. This will provide consumers with a national help-line providing consumers with information on their rights and practical advice on their problems.
- Second, there may be a continuing movement toward multi-utility providers. In these cases, customer interface in relation to a number of services is with a single company such as Centrica or United Utilities.
- Third, utility markets in particular share a common customer base.

Each of these factors, together with the ongoing need to ensure that consumer representation is provided efficiently and effectively, means that there is a continuing and increasing requirement to exploit synergies for consumer representative bodies.

8.6 These drivers are important influences of the medium-term vision set out in this report and underpin its recommendations. However, there may be significant additional benefits from organising consumer representation functionally rather than by sector. This scenario would witness the establishment of a single consumer body responsible for consumer advocacy across a number of sectors. This is not a new concept. In 1997, Consumers Association recommended establishing a Public Utilities Consumer Council to cover water, electricity and gas. Another model which has been looked at during the review is illustrated in Figure 3.

8.7 This delivery model would promote:
- increased flexibility in responding to market changes over time;
- economies of scale and scope to be realised;
- one consumer advocacy body to represent consumers with regard to these essential services;
- a stronger voice by which to influence policy in the UK and EU;
- increased incentives on companies to resolve complaints at source.

8.8 However, this scenario also highlights features of current arrangements that are of value and would need to be incorporated into any alternative arrangements. These include maintaining sectoral expertise, perhaps through distinct teams that deal with sector specific policy issues; use of complaints information to inform strategic decision-making and close links between regional representation and central decision-making.

Figure 3: Possible future scenario for consumer representation in utility markets

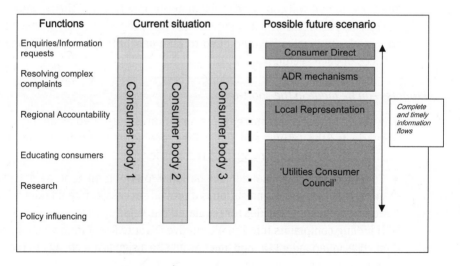

8.9 This model would allow consumer representation to be strengthened by having one organisation that could draw on the experience of consumer representation across the spectrum of markets in areas, such as consumer empowerment, and could conduct cross-cutting research into consumer behaviour.

8.10 As Chapter 6 illustrated, some of the consumer bodies have a statutory duty to handle unresolved consumer complaints. This is an expensive and time-consuming function for these small organisations. Under the new model, it may not be necessary for the unitary organisation to be responsible for handling unresolved consumer complaints. Alternative dispute resolution (ADRs) arrangements can provide an alternative delivery mechanism for consumer redress. In particular, ADRs can ensure that the appropriate incentives are in place to provide companies with the appropriate incentives to resolve consumer complaints quickly and effectively. The introduction of ADR's however, should only accompany a consolidation of existing consumer bodies so as to avoid a proliferation of bodies with overlapping remits in regulated markets. Such a proliferation would not be in the consumer's interest, nor would it be efficient.

8.11 This new model is not a statement of Government policy, and this study has not undertaken a full policy assessment of this new approach. Nonetheless, there are strong drivers for change in the medium to long term. As a result, as part of a consultation on the Government's proposed Consumer Strategy, the Government will consult on this longer-term vision and the potential for ADRs. Any proposals which emerged from this process, including which sectors might be involved, would need to take account of the specific circumstances of each sector.

Progress can be made in the short-term

8.12 The above model of consumer representation is presented as an indicative scenario for the future, and not a firm recommendation for institutional change now. There are a number of reasons for this:

- Consumer Direct will not achieve national roll-out until 2006-07. It will be important that this organisation is a proven success before it takes on any additional responsibilities for regulated markets[34].
- Handling complaints through Alternative Dispute Resolution mechanisms, such as independent Ombudsmen, would be a significant change to the current arrangements with implications for regulators, industry and consumers. Otelo has only recently been established and still has to be proven.

---

34 The first wave of Consumer Direct regions will – by end 2004 – have provided substantial validation of the basic operational model. However, in respect of the formal transfer of national functions – such as the handling of first tier enquiries and advice – the delay before national roll-out of the service may act as a constraint on a move towards a new operating model for the consumer bodies.

- There has been significant organisational change for some of the consumer bodies in recent years, particularly in energy, post and water. It is important not to de-stabilise the system for consumer representation unnecessarily.

8.13 Moreover, a number of steps are beginning to be taken by the consumer bodies to deliver some of the benefits of joint working. The Government warmly welcomes the recent initiative by energywatch and Postwatch to set up a consumer forum – the Consumer Action Network. This forum will help identify and act upon synergies and potential efficiency gains from joint activity. Its priorities at present focus on operational Issues. The Government has a part to play in ensuring that the policy framework that supports these bodies does not hold back progress in this area. The Consumer Action Network is also a forum from which best practice can be shared and collective knowledge of consumers pooled. There may also be scope for the forum to be usefully used for policy issues. One could envisage sector specific consumer bodies developing and launching joint campaigns where appropriate, for example on consumer rights or debt issues.

Recommendation 10

Consumer bodies should continue to explore ways in which to exploit synergies from joint working.

- The Consumer Action Network is an important vehicle for delivering this and should:
    - identify 2-3 key initiatives to take forward over coming months that will deliver real benefits; and
    - concentrate on both operational issues and delivery of consumer representation. For example consumer empowerment and joint procurement of some common functions such as legal resource.
- Sectoral consumer bodies should review opportunities for savings through partnering with other organisations with a view to outsourcing certain 'back office' functions collaboratively, based on common process, in order to obtain benefits of scale.
- Evaluate scope for partnering with other organisations to provide key functions including if appropriate complaints handling and campaigning.

Summary of recommendations

The following is a high-level summary of the main recommendations.

- Consumer bodies should target resources where they will have maximum impact.
- Consumer bodies and their spending teams should work together to develop meaningful measures of performance.
- The super-complaint provisions of the Enterprise Act provide opportunities for consumer bodies and regulators. Postwatch and the new Consumer Council for Water should apply for super-complaint status. (Energywatch applied in February 2004).
- Consumer bodies should work together to develop a new strategy for complaint handling on the following principles:
  - Companies should bear primary responsibility for handling complaints efficiently and effectively;
  - Consumer Direct will become the one-stop shop for all first tier consumer enquiries;
  - Complaints handling by consumer bodies should be further consolidated regionally (i.e. outside London and the South East) within each body.
- Consumer bodies must ensure that regional representation continues to offer good value for money.
- Consumer bodies should work closely with other stakeholders to increase consumer empowerment.
- Consumer bodies should deepen and strengthen their strategic partnerships with regulators and Government.
- Consumer bodies should engage strategically with companies to deliver better outcomes for consumers.
- Consumer bodies should continue to explore ways in which to exploit synergies from joint working.
- Consumer bodies should seek full engagement at the EU level, whether alone or through joint action with other consumer bodies; regulators; and Government.

Anhang

Vertretung von Verbraucherinteressen in regulierten Märkten –
Informationen zur Situation in Großbritannien und Deutschland

1. Das britische Modell der consumer watchdogs

Um der Stimme der Verbraucher in liberalisierten Märkten Gewicht zu verleihen, sind in Großbritannien sogenannte consumer watchdogs, das sind spezialisierte Verbraucherorganisationen für jeden der liberalisierten Märkte, gegründet worden.

1.1. Die Consumer Watchdogs

Es gibt hierbei zwei verschiedene Organisationsmodelle. Die meisten der watchdogs sind der jeweiligen Regulierungsbehörde organisatorisch zugeordnet, andere sind von diesen unabhängig. Die folgenden Tabellen listen die einzelnen watchdogs gegliedert nach ihrer Organisationsform auf:

Watchdogs im Geschäftsbereich der Regulierungsbehörden

Name, Gründungsjahr, Internetadresse	Zuständigkeit	Regulierungsbehörde des jeweiligen Sektors
OFCOM Consumer Panel, 2003 http://www.ofcomconsumerpanel.org.uk	Telekommunikation, Fernsehen und Hörfunk	Office of Communications (OFCOM)
WaterVoice, 1991 http://www.watervoice.org.uk	Wasserversorgung	Office of Water Services (Ofwat)
Financial Services Consumer Panel, 1997 http://www.fsa.gov.uk	Finanzdienstleistungen	Financial Services Authority (FSA)
Air Transport Users Council (AUC), 1973 http://www.caa.co.uk/auc	Flugreisen	Civil Aviation Authority (CAA)
Rail Passengers Council, 2000 http://www.railpassengers.org.uk	Bahnreisen	Strategic Rail Authority (SRA)

Unabhängige watchdogs

Name, Gründungsjahr, Internetadresse	Zuständigkeit	Regulierungsbehörde des jeweiligen Sektors
Energywatch, 2000 http://www.energywatch.org.uk	Strom und Gas	Office of Gas and Electricity Markets (Ofgem)
Postwatch, 2001 http://www.postwatch.co.uk	Postdienstleistungen	Postal Services Commission (Postcomm)

1.2. Aufgabe der Watchdogs

Die Aufgabe der *Watchdogs* ist es, gegenüber der Politik und gegenüber den Unternehmen die Interessen der Verbraucher zu vertreten. Die *Watchdogs* sind zu diesem Zweck ausdrücklich in den jeweiligen Fachgesetzen verankert. Die Vertretung der Verbraucherinteressen findet auf zwei Ebenen statt:

- **auf politischer Ebene**, indem sich die *Watchdogs* gegenüber den Regulierungsbehörden und gegenüber dem Gesetzgeber für eine verbrauchergerechte Marktordnung einsetzen, und

- **auf individueller Ebene**, indem die watchdogs den Beschwerden von einzelnen Verbrauchern nachgehen.

Auf der **politischen Ebene** setzen die watchdogs Medienarbeit ebenso ein wie eine konstruktive Zusammenarbeit mit Behörden und Unternehmen. Zusätzlich steht ihnen mit dem *Supercomplaint* ein besonderes Druckmittel zur Verfügung. Hiernach können anerkannte Verbraucherorganisationen beim *Office of Fair Trading* (OFT) eine Beschwerde einreichen, wenn die Interessen der Verbraucher in einem Markt erheblich beeinträchtigt werden. Das *Office of Fair Trading* ist eine Behörde, die durch die Verfolgung von Rechtsverstößen, durch Verbraucherinformationen und durch politische Initiativen für eine verbrauchergerechte Wettbewerbsordnung sorgt (http://www.oft.gov.uk). Das OFT ist verpflichtet, auf einen *Supercomplaint* innerhalb von 90 Tagen zu antworten und darzulegen, ob und gegebenenfalls welche Maßnahmen es ergreifen wird, um der Beschwerde abzuhelfen.

Individuelle Beschwerden werden von den meisten, aber nicht von allen *Watchdogs* bearbeitet. Bei zwei Watchdogs (OFCOM *Consumer Panel* und *FSA Consumer Panel*), die der Regulierungsbehörde direkt zugeordnet sind, ist die Aufgabe der Beschwerdebearbeitung dagegen ausgelagert. Hier existieren außergerichtliche Streitschlichtungsstellen, die von den *Watchdogs* institutionell unabhängig sind, der Financial Ombudsman Service (http://www.financial-ombudsman.org.uk) und Otelo, der Ombudsmann im Bereich Telekommunikation (http://www.otelo.org.uk). Diese verstehen sich nicht als Interessenvertretung der Verbraucher, sondern als neutrale Schiedsstellen. Je nachdem, ob die Beschwerden von den watchdogs selbst oder von Ombudsstellen bearbeitet werden, unterscheidet sich auch das Verfahren. Die watchdogs setzen zur Lösung von Beschwerdefällen auf die öffentliche Aufmerksamkeit und auf den Kontakt zu den Regulierungsbehörden. Die Ombudsstellen dagegen entscheiden über die Beschwerden in einem gerichtsähnlichen Verfahren. Die Entscheidungen binden das betroffene Unternehmen, nicht aber den Verbraucher, der die Beschwerde eingelegt hat. Dem Verbraucher bleibt die Möglichkeit, durch Klage vor den ordentlichen Gerichten eine andere Lösung zu erstreiten.

1.3. Ausstattung und Finanzierung der watchdogs

Die fünf wichtigsten *Watchdogs*[1] verfügten in den Jahren 2002/2003[2] über ein durchschnittliches Jahresbudget von knapp 25 Millionen Pfund (38 Millionen Euro) und beschäftigten mehr als 800 Mitarbeiter in 27 Niederlassungen. Einige der watchdogs verfügen über ein Netz von acht bis zehn Regionalbüros und Regionalkomitees *(Postwatch, Energywatch, WaterVoice, Rail Passenger Council)*. In den Jahren 2002/2003 behandelten die *Watchdogs* 164.000 Beschwerden und beantworteten mehr als 115.000 Verbraucheranfragen.

Die Aufsichtsbefugnisse und die finanziellen Beziehungen sind unterschiedlich organisiert; je nachdem, ob der *Watchdog* in die Regulierungsbehörde eingegliedert oder von dieser unabhängig ist. Die unabhängigen *Watchdogs*, also Energywatch und Postwatch, werden direkt vom Handels- und Industrieministerium (Departement of Trade and Industry, DTI) finanziert; sie sind alleine diesem direkt verantwortlich. Die bei den Regulierungsbehörden angesiedelten *Watchdogs* werden direkt aus deren Etat finanziert und unterliegen einer weiterreichenden inhaltlichen Kontrolle. Beim *Air Transport Users Council* (AUC) setzt sich die Finanzierung je zur Hälfte aus beiden Elementen (Unternehmensgebühren und direkte Finanzierung aus dem Behördenetat) zusammen.

2. Vertretung von Verbraucherinteressen in liberalisierten Märkten – die Situation in Deutschland

In Deutschland existiert unter dem Dach des Verbraucherzentrale Bundesverbandes ein Netz von Verbraucherorganisationen, das strukturell geeignet ist, die Vertretung von Verbraucherinteressen in den liberalisierten Märkten zu leisten. Die Verbraucherzentralen der Länder sowie spezialisierte Verbraucherorganisationen wie zum Beispiel die Mieterschutzvereine beraten die Verbraucher bei individuellen Beschwerden. Der Verbraucherzentrale Bundesverband erfüllt als bundesweite Dachorganisation eine doppelte Funktion: Zum einen koordiniert er die Arbeit der Verbraucherverbände und stellt ein Kommunikationsnetzwerk für den Austausch zwischen Dachverband und den dezentralen Mitgliedsverbänden zur Verfügung. Zum anderen setzt er sich auf politischer Ebene für die Interessen der Verbraucher

---

1 Von den vorgenannten Verbraucherorganisationen bleiben bei den folgenden Daten ausgespart: das OFCOM Consumer Panel, das erst im Jahr 2004 eingerichtet wurde, und das Rail Passenger Council, das eine besondere Funktion im Bahnsektor einnimmt; Quelle: Evaluierungsbericht von DTI und HM Treasury, http://www.dti.gov.uk/ccp/topics1/pdf1/cpeconreport.pdf.
2 Daten für den Zeitraum 1.04.2002 bis 31.03.2003; Quelle: Evaluierungsbericht von DTI und HM Treasury, http://www.dti.gov.uk/ccp/topics1/pdf1/cpeconreport.pdf.

ein und sorgt auf diese Weise dafür, dass die Marktkenntnis der einzelnen Verbraucherorganisationen auch in den politischen Prozess Eingang findet. Die Verbraucherverbände verfügen darüber hinaus über Klagerechte, um im Fall von Wettbewerbsverstößen die Interessen der Verbraucher auch gerichtlich durchzusetzen.

Allerdings mangelt es in Deutschland sowohl an besonderen rechtlichen Vorkehrungen für die Verbrauchervertretung in den liberalisierten Märkten als auch an der erforderlichen finanziellen Ausstattung der Verbraucherorganisationen, um die neuen verbraucherpolitischen Herausforderungen der liberalisierten Versorgungsmärkte anzugehen. In Großbritannien folgte der Liberalisierung mit dem Aufbau des Systems der watchdogs eine Phase des verbraucherpolitischen Aufbruchs. In Deutschland dagegen werden die Kapazitäten der Verbraucherzentralen derzeit massiv abgebaut. Im laufenden Gesetzesverfahren für ein neues Energiewirtschaftsgesetz spielt die Organisation und Finanzierung der Verbraucherinteressen keine Rolle.

Die Autoren

Allan Asher

Chief Executive von *Energywatch*, der unabhängigen *Watchdog*-Organsiation, die Verbraucherinteressen auf dem Energiemarkt vertritt. Zuvor Leiter der Abteilung Kampagnen und Öffentlichkeitsarbeit der *Consumers' Association* und Mitglied des Führungsstabs. Verschiedene Tätigkeiten für den Weltverbraucherverband Consumers International.

Edward Blades

Seit 2003 im *Economic Regulation Team* im Britischen Handels- und Industrieministerium (*Department of Trade and Industry*, DTI) tätig. Vorher *Head of Electricity and Gas Regulation Policy* im DTI. Viele Jahre im Privatisierungsprogramm des Vereinigten Königreiches tätig, unter anderem beteiligt am Aufbau von gemeinsamen Projekten zwischen *British Steel* und dem privaten Sektor.

Anja Dobrodinsky

Freie Journalistin, 2004/2005 Teilnehmerin von „*Praxis*[4]" des Traineeprogramms für Verbraucherjournalisten.

Gregor McGregor

Chief Executive von Postwatch, der Verbraucherorganisation, die Postdienstleister im Vereinigten Königreich beobachtet. Postwatch überwacht Zustellung, Dienstleistungsstandards, Preise und Wettbewerb auf dem Postmarkt. Zuvor war Gregor McGregor Leiter der Abteilung Wettbewerb und Regulierung der *Postal Services Commission* (Postcomm) und Chef der Abteilung Politik- und Regierungsbeziehungen bei Railtrack.

Prof. Dr. Edda Müller

Seit 2001 Vorstand des Verbraucherzentrale Bundesverbandes. Stellvertretende Vorsitzende des Rats für Nachhaltige Entwicklung und Mitglied im Verwaltungsrat der Stiftung Warentest. 1998 bis 2000 Vizedirektorin der Europäischen Umweltagentur in Kopenhagen, zuvor Leiterin der Abteilung Klimapolitik des Wuppertal

Instituts für Klima, Umwelt und Energie und Ministerin für Natur und Umwelt in Schleswig-Holstein.

Sheila Reiter

Seit 1995 Vorsitzende von *WaterVoice Wessex*, Großbritannien und Mitglied des WaterVoice Council, die politische Interessenvertretung von Wasserkunden in Großbritannien. *WaterVoice Wessex* vertritt die Interessen der Verbraucher in vier der 25 Wassergesellschaften in England und Wales. Außerdem ist Sheila Reiter stellvertretende Vorsitzende der *National Health Service Logistics Authority* und ehemalige *Justice of the Peace*.

Dr. Alois Rhiel

Minister für Wirtschaft, Verkehr und Landesentwicklung in Hessen. Zuvor Bürgermeister der Stadt Fulda, Regierungspräsident in Gießen, stellvertretender Vorsitzender des Vorstands der Tegut-Lebensmittelgruppe. Seit 1992 Mitglied im Landesvorstand der CDU Hessen, Präsidiumsmitglied im Hessischen Städtetag, Präsidiumsmitglied der Deutschen Gartenbaugesellschaft.

Dr. Franz-Georg Rips

Seit 1995 Direktor des Deutschen Mieterbundes. Gleichzeitig Geschäftsführer des DMB-Verlages und Vorstandssprecher der DMB-Rechtsschutz-Versicherung AG. Stellvertretender Vorsitzender des Verwaltungsrates des Verbraucherzentrale Bundesverbands, zuvor Vorsitzender (2000 bis 2003). Mitglied des Vorstandes des Mietervereins Köln. Zuvor Bürgermeister von Erftstadt. Von 2002 bis 2004 Mitglied der Expertenkommission Wohnungsgenossenschaften der Bundesregierung.

Sabine Streb

Seit 2001 wissenschaftliche Mitarbeiterin der Monopolkommission, einem unabhängigen Expertengremium zur Begutachtung der Wettbewerbsentwicklung in der Bundesrepublik und zur Beratung der Bundesregierung in Fragen der Wettbewerbspolitik. Aufgabengebiete: kartellrechtliche Fallpraxis, Regulierung, Energiewirtschaft. Zuvor wissenschaftliche Mitarbeiterin der Universität Heidelberg, Lehrstuhl für internationale Wirtschafts- und Entwicklungspolitik. Diplomvolkswirtin.

Dr. Jorge Vasconcelos

Mitbegründer und Vorsitzender des Rats der Europäischen Energie-Regulierer (CEER). Vorsitzender von ERSE, der Regulierungsbehörde der portugiesischen Elektrizitäts- und Gasindustrie. Zuvor in der Abteilung Elektrische Netzwerke von AEG in Frankfurt tätig, stellvertretender Generalsekretär von EURELECTRIC *(European Association of Electricity Industry)* und Gastprofessor an der Universität von Pavia, Italien. Seit 2001 hält er auch Vorlesungen an der Universität von Coimbra, Portugal.

Prof. Dr. Helmut Voelzkow

Seit 2002 Professor für international vergleichende Sozialwissenschaften an der Universität Osnabrück. Zuvor Dozent an der Universität Bochum. Von 1996 bis 2002 forschte er am Max-Planck-Institut für Gesellschaftsforschung Köln auf den Gebieten ökonomische Soziologie, vergleichende Sozial- und Politikwissenschaften, europäische Integration und institutionelle Theorie.

Band 1 Verbraucherzentrale Bundesverband e.V. (vzbv) (Hrsg.)
Verbraucherforschung in Deutschland
Die heutige Verbraucherforschung ist zersplittert und weist erhebliche Forschungslücken auf. Es fehlt an einer interdisziplinären Zusammenführung der sektoralen Forschungsthemen, auch einen Lehrstuhl für Verbraucherpolitik gibt es nicht. Die neue Verbraucherpolitik braucht aber einen theoretischen Überbau und eine wissenschaftliche Fundierung, die die Bemühungen um bessere Bedingungen der Verbraucherpolitik im politischen Prozess unterstützt. Politik und Wissenschaft müssen die Bedeutung einer verbraucher- und verbraucherpolitisch orientierten Forschung künftig stärker erkennen. Diesem Zweck dient die vorliegende Veröffentlichung. Wir suchen mit ihr den Dialog über notwendige Maßnahmen mit Wissenschaftlern der verschiedenen Disziplinen und mit den Akteuren in Wissenschaftsinstitutionen und Forschungsförderung.
2005, 304 S., kart., 45,60 Euro, ISBN 3-8305-0925-1

Band 2 Hans-W. Micklitz
Bauverträge mit Verbrauchern und die VOB Teil B
Zur Bedeutung der Richtlinie 93/13/EWG über
missbräuchliche Klauseln in Verbraucherverträgen
Das deutsche private Baurecht wird von der Vergabe- und Vertragsordnung für Bauleistungen Teil B regiert. Dabei handelt es sich um allgemeine Geschäftsbedingungen, die ursprünglich für die Abwicklung öffentlicher Bauaufträge entwickelt wurden und unmodifiziert auch auf Bauverträge mit Verbrauchern angewandt werden. Gesetzgebung und Rechtsprechung haben mit der Theorie der Ausgewogenheit der VOB/B als Ganzes einen Schutzwall gezogen. Eine gesetzliche Kontrolle, ob die Inhalte der VOB/B auch verbrauchergerecht sind, ist seit 1977 ausgeschaltet.
Das vorliegende Rechtsgutachten zeigt, dass die Freistellung der VOB/B von einer gesetzlichen Kontrolle mit der EG-Richtlinie 93/13/EWG über missbräuchliche Klauseln in Verbraucherverträgen unvereinbar ist und die VOB/B 2002 eine Vielzahl von Klauseln enthält, die private Bauherren unangemessen benachteiligen. Von Ausgewogenheit bei Verbraucherverträgen keine Spur.
2005, 219 S., kart., 29,80 Euro, ISBN 3-8305-0861-1

BERLINER WISSENSCHAFTS-VERLAG GmbH
Axel-Springer-Str. 54 b • 10117 Berlin • Tel. 030 / 84 17 70-0 • Fax 030 / 84 17 70-21
E-Mail: bwv@bwv-verlag.de • http://www.bwv-verlag.de

Band 3 Verbraucherzentrale Bundesverband e.V. (vzbv) (Hrsg.)
„PISA" in der Verbraucherbildung
Sind wir alle Konsum-Analphabeten?

Mit seiner Tagung „Pisa in der Verbraucherbildung" hat der Verbraucherzentrale Bundesverband eine Offensive für eine Reform der Verbraucherbildung an unseren Schulen gestartet. Eigenverantwortung im Konsum – dieses Ziel der Bildungspolitik wird derzeit kaum erreicht. Stattdessen ist ein zunehmender Konsum-Analphabetismus zu beobachten. Die hier versammelten Beiträge zielen auf eine Schule, die Schülerinnen und Schüler auf ein Leben als Bürger und Konsumenten vorbereitet. In einer solchen Schule können Kinder und Jugendliche „intelligente Lebensstile" lernen, sich mit Fragen einer gesunden Ernährung und Lebensweise, der finanziellen Alltagswirklichkeit oder des ressourcenschonenden Konsums auseinandersetzen. Die Ergebnisse einer Schulbuchanalyse zum Thema Finanzdienstleistungen komplettieren diesen Band.

2005, 184 S., kart., 28,80 Euro, ISBN 3-8305-0926-X

Band 4 Verbraucherzentrale Bundesverband e.V. (vzbv) (Hrsg.)
Wirtschaftsfaktor Verbraucherinformation
Die Bedeutung von Informationen für funktionierende Märkte

Marktwirtschaft kann nur funktionieren, wenn Verbraucher sich als Marktteilnehmer rational verhalten können. Sie müssen Zugang zu denjenigen Informationen haben, die für ihre Entscheidung beim Kauf von Waren und der Inanspruchnahme von Dienstleistungen relevant sind. Die Forschungen der Nobelpreisträger Akerlof, Spence und Stiglitz zeigen auf, welche dramatischen Folgen für die Märkte „asymmetrische Informationen" haben können, was also geschieht, wenn eine Seite des Marktes über bedeutend weniger Informationen verfügt als die andere.

In den Beiträgen zu der Veranstaltung „Was Verbraucher wissen wollen – Wirtschaftsfaktor Verbraucherinformation" vom 17.06.2004 wird deutlich, wie sehr es gerade der Wirtschaft darum gehen muss, die Verbraucher möglichst umfassend über Produkt- und Prozessqualitäten von Waren und Dienstleistungen zu informieren.

2005, 151 S., kart., 24,– Euro, ISBN 3-8305-1010-1

BERLINER WISSENSCHAFTS-VERLAG GmbH
Axel-Springer-Str. 54 b • 10117 Berlin • Tel. 030 / 84 17 70-0 • Fax 030 / 84 17 70-21
E-Mail: bwv@bwv-verlag.de • http://www.bwv-verlag.de